Finding the Favor of God is not a blessing Ronnie Floyd writes about in the third person. He has found the favor of God by beating out on the anvil of personal experience a lifetime of integrity in ministry. Who doesn't want the favor of God? This volume is for anyone anywhere who has discovered that it is greater to be a blessing than to get a blessing. Read it and reap!

O.S. Hawkins

Ronnie Floyd is a faithful and visionary pastor, who desperately desires to see his people grow to understand the meaning of the gospel and the reality of God's grace. *Finding the Favor of God* reflects Ronnie Floyd's heart, mind, and soul. This is a pastor who lives what he teaches.

R. Albert Mohler Jr.
President, The Southern Baptist Theological Seminary
Louisville, KY

Ronnie not only helps us to understand the favor of God but how to experience it in every dimension of our lives as we yield ourselves to Him. This is an essential read for the entire church family.

Dr. Tom Mullins, Senior Pastor, Christ Fellowship Church

I've heard Dr. Floyd preach on the subject of "finding the favor of God." It was apparent that much research had been done and that God had blessed in his discovery. Read these marvelous pages and begin to experience that favor of God as you apply the principles. It is a "must read."

Dr. Johnny M. Hunt
First Baptist Church, Woodstock, GA

It is my opinion that favor is better than labor and that one day of favor can save a leader a month of labor. In Dr. Ronnie Floyd's remarkable book, he shows the pathway for us to multiply our efforts through seeking God's favor in our lives and applying it to a lost and dying world. I highly recommend this dynamic resource to leaders who wish to find God's favor in both Christian and non-Christian arenas today.

Dr. James O. Davis
Co-founder/President/CEO, Global Pastor's Network

Ronnie Floyd communicates with today's generation better than anyone I know. Don't miss his newest book, *Finding The Favor of God*. It will help you in your search for God's best in your life.

Dr. Jerry Falwell, Founder and Chancellor
Liberty University, Lynchburg, VA

Over 20 years ago, I heard an evangelist define *grace* as the unmerited favor of God. That caused me to begin thinking and learning more about God's favor. As one who has been favored by God, I eagerly awaited *Finding the Favor of God*, by Dr. Ronnie Floyd. It did not disappoint! As you read it, I pray that you, too, will find increased favor from God.

John A. White, Ph.D.
Chancellor, University of Arkansas

In Psalm 103:7, the Scripture says, "He [God] made known his ways to Moses, his acts to the children of Israel." Ronnie Floyd continues to explore and share the "ways" of God. The body of Christ is blessed by Ronnie's journey.

Barbara O'Chester

This book is a gift to every modern-day Jacob who won't let go until he finds God's favor. Once you read these pages, you will never again be content to settle, but only to soar.

Jay H. Strack,
President, www.studentleadership.net

God has gifted Ronnie Floyd with a wonderful ability to communicate significant truths from His word. I commend his new book, *Finding the Favor of God,* as a significant contribution in the journey of faith that we, as believers, have begun. It will be a blessing, a challenge, an inspiration, and an immeasurable contribution to your life. I commend it to you with sincere prayer for God's blessings upon your life as you read these pages.

James T. Draper, Jr.
President, LifeWay

Finding The Favor of God has made an impact on my entire family. We are excited about the wonderful news of asking for the favor of God. I believe God has given Ronnie Floyd His favor.

Houston Nutt
Head Football Coach, University of Arkansas

Once again my friend Ronnie Floyd has done a masterful job of motivating believers on their walk with the Lord. *Finding the Favor of God* will enrich your relationship with the Father as you read of the biblical heroes and the everyday people of faith who have experienced God's favor. Dig into its pages and search for yourself. You will discover treasure that will change your life.

Dr. Ed Young, Pastor
Second Baptist Church, Houston, TX

With a penchant for turning up the unusual approach in God's Word, Dr. Ronnie Floyd has penned a challenging book on a subject heretofore almost totally neglected. *Finding the Favor of God — A Discovery That Will Change Your Life*, the title of the book, is almost an understatement. Finding God's favor, as explicated on these pages, is, indeed, the only thing that brings significance and happiness to life.

Dr. Paige Patterson, President
Southwestern Baptist Theological Seminary, Fort Worth, TX

I know that I have experienced the favor of God, even though I wasn't aware I was asking for it. One of my life's verses is James 4:8, "Draw near to God and He will draw near to you." In this book, Pastor Floyd sets out specifically how you can best draw near to God and therefore by His grace, experience His favor in drawing near to you.

Norm Miller, Chairman of the Board
Interstate Battery System of America, Inc.

Finding the Favor of GOD

A Discovery That Will Change Your Life

Dr. Ronnie Floyd

Printed in the United States of America

Please visit our website for other great titles:
www.newleafpress.net

For information regarding author interviews,
please contact the publicity department at (870) 438-5288.

New Leaf Press
A Division of New Leaf Publishing Group

DEDICATION

"Remember me, my God, with favor."
(Neh. 13:31)

Thank You

My heart is full of gratitude to the following persons who have contributed to this work:

Jeana, my life-partner, who always sacrifices voluntarily for me to share words of life with people.

Josh, Kate, Nick, and Meredith, thanks for the way you are positioning your lives already to receive the favor of God, and apparently His gaze is already on you in many ways.

Chris Johnson, my ministry assistant, who helped me with some initial research over two years ago.

Gayla Oldham and Melissa Swain, my assistants, who have supplied encouragement and the completion of details for many areas of this project.

Dr. Alan Damron, one of my associate pastors, who brainstormed with me on many of these ideas and thoughts.

Craig Pulley, our Executive Director of Invitation to Life, who always challenges us to synergize our forces to get the message out to the people.

Steve Halliday, a gifted writer and collaborator who helped me place many of these thoughts, concepts, illustrations, and biblical principles onto the page.

Jim Fletcher, an editor with New Leaf Press, who worked with me through this project and its completion.

Tim Dudley, president of New Leaf Press, a friend and a man who believes in this message and messenger.

Entire New Leaf Press team, thanks for assisting and believing in me as we partner to share God's favor with the world through the publication of this work.

You, the reader, the most important person of all, may the favor of the Lord be upon you as He fixes His gaze upon you, even the details of your life.

To all of you: Thanks and may the favor of the Lord our God be with you and bless the work of our hands, yes, the work of our hands!

CONTENTS

Introduction

The Favor of God and You

As a teenage boy growing up in the heat and humidity of southwest Texas, I used to dream about becoming a football coach. I loved the game. I loved everything that went with the game — the preparation, the competition, the Friday night lights, and, most of all, winning. I felt destined to become a football coach.

But things changed one year during the months of February and March, just as we began to practice for track and field. More to the point, I changed.

Dripping with sweat after running laps or sprints, I would stop to meditate on what I should do with my life. Where was I going? What should I do? My formerly insatiable passion to coach football began to wane as God put something new and different on my heart. I made my decision within weeks. Suddenly I had a clear direction and a new life course.

Like everyone else, however, I could not know what a marvelous adventure God had in store for me.

*A*bout two years ago, I began carefully investigating the subject, "the favor of God." I found it fascinating that not many books consider the topic. In fact, have you ever seen an entire book written on the favor of God? I had not until the one I wrote for you.

Yet the Bible speaks a great deal about favor. The more I listened to what God's Word says about finding His favor, the more passionate I have become about it.

Why do I feel such passion about this subject?

First, because I've witnessed something in my own life that clearly had nothing to do with giftedness or ability. Something unique and dramatic in my spiritual life has occurred, and in a mysterious manner.

Second, when I began reading through the Bible annually back in 1990, I began seeing the phrase "the favor of God" throughout the Scriptures. Even before I made a special study of the phrase, it so intrigued me that I began to seek God to give me His favor. As a result God, has been doing exactly that.

Third, I began to witness that certain people often get placed in significant places of spiritual influence that, frankly, seem to make no sense. I put myself in this category. Why would God determine to place this guy, who grew up in a church of 30–40 people in weekly attendance, into the kind of church I serve today? There are better leaders, better communicators, and better people — so why me? That question has motivated me to explore more about the favor of God, and what God sees in me that I may not be able to see.

Fourth, I have noticed that the practice of certain spiritual disciplines seems to clear the way for the favor of God to arrive. I came to Christ during my sophomore year in high school. I did not become perfect, but things began to change. I still made some mistakes, but my whole life got turned upside-down, and I began to pursue the things of God with great eagerness. I soon realized that I needed to develop healthy patterns and spiritual disciplines such as regular prayer and spending time in the Word, and such habits have helped me to become more of what God wants me to be. When I entered college, I began to pursue the discipline of fasting, which seemed to take God's favor to a whole new level. Even though I didn't understand it at the time, I now look back and say, *"Oh, yes! God seems to use certain disciplines to position His children for receiving His favor."*

♦ ♦ ♦ GETTING PASSIONATE ♦ ♦ ♦

In this book, I'd like to motivate you to get passionate about seeking the favor of God for yourself. Probably you have heard the phrase, but perhaps you have never explored its meaning or its personal ramifications. I want to help you get started connecting the dots. I want you to see that you can experience the favor of God.

By the end of our short time together, I'd like for you to be able to say, "This is really incredible! You mean it's okay for me to pray for the favor of God? How do I do that? What do I do?"

Consider this book a word of hope. God can take you, regardless of where you've been in your life — bad, good, worthy, unworthy — and show you His favor. Your age nor your spiritual background matters. Why? Because God's favor does not depend on your credentials. Remember, you won't be reading merely about how other people or somebody else received God's favor. *You* can have God's favor!

♦ ♦ ♦ EXPERIENCE GOD'S FAVOR ♦ ♦ ♦

The favor of God is as important as it is unexplored and misunderstood. Both the Old and the New Testaments frequently highlight God's favor. Heroes of faith such as Moses, David, Daniel, Mary, Peter, Paul, and others both discovered and experienced the favor of God. You can, too.

While a certain mystery will always color the favor of God, it can be sought after, discovered, experienced, and enjoyed. Favor is not a toy to play with nor a blessing to exploit. While complete understanding of God's favor will remain forever beyond our grasp, we can do much to find it and experience it.

Starting today!

PART ONE

WHAT IS GOD'S FAVOR?

When James Scantlin talked to his daughter, Sarah, on the phone one winter day in early 2005, he considered it a miracle. Now, most daddies will tell you that talking to their little girls is always wonderful, but it was especially true in James's case.

Sarah, you see, had been in a coma for 20 years. The victim of a hit-and-run accident in 1984, she'd been lost to her family and friends for a staggering two decades. Medical professionals usually tell the loved ones of such cases what all of us intuitively understand: long-term comas almost always end badly.

When Sarah Scantlin began reading a children's book that her nurse was showing her "for the pictures," pandemonium broke out. Phone calls, visits, and joy unspeakable followed. Sarah gradually began recovering her memory and recognized friends who had aged 20 years.

Thousands of patients in Sarah's condition will never wake up. So her re-entry into this world begs the question: Why was she favored with a second chance?

What is the favor of God? Why should we want it? How can having the favor of God spell the difference between success and failure, hope and despair, joy and regret? In this section, as we look into what the Bible says about the favor of God, seeking to gain a solid scriptural understanding, it will enable us to begin a personal journey overflowing with His good favor.

GRASPING THE FAVOR OF GOD

1

I walked into the student center just as she walked out. I couldn't help but look, and felt an immediate attraction to this lovely young woman. Yet I was a second semester freshman, and I soon discovered she had been there longer than I. Could this slight difference in age put an end to the dreams I already had? I knew it might stop her, but I would not let it stop me.

Happily, it did not stop either of us. Our dates to the local Sonic drive-in and our late-night walks around the campus became frequent. The favor of God was kicking in.

By the next semester, I found myself falling in love with her. Howard Payne University in Brownwood, Texas, served as the place where God brought together a west Texas girl with this south Texas boy. On December 31, 1976, Jeana and I got married.

Although not all of our 28 years of marriage have been easy by a long shot, we never considered an alternative. Not once did we stubbornly refuse to work out our issues or allow killer conflicts to burrow deep into our hearts and begin their destructive work.

Even as I write this book, I'm happy to report that God has given both of us a renewal of honeymoon love. I've never experienced more unconditional, sacrificial, and willing love for my wife. I sense that we're walking in an unusual season of marital life, and it thrills me. After almost 29 years together, we are empty nesters — and we love it. We loved being together before the kids ever came along, and we love it now that they've left.

What causes something so wonderful as this? What enables us to enjoy it? Nothing but the favor of God.

♦ ♦ ♦ FAVOR AND YOUR MARRIAGE ♦ ♦ ♦

What about your marriage? Does love flourish? Do you still feel honeymoon love, or does that seem impossible? The favor of God can change any marriage. You might not have started out right, or it may not be right even now, but His favor can change everything.

When we started having children, Jeana felt very concerned about creating an environment that would encourage our kids to love the Lord and His church. As a pastor's kid herself, she knew that many PKs (pastor's kids) struggle on both counts. Even before our children were born (and continuing yet today), we prayed that the Lord would give our boys a heart for God.

When people would ask, "How can I pray for you and your family?" I would always reply, "Pray that my sons will grow up loving Christ and loving the church." And you know what? The Lord has answered those prayers! So far as we know, Josh never had a moment of rebellion against God. Today, he's married to a lovely girl named Kate who also loves Christ. Nick is beginning seminary, studying to be a pastor. He just married a wonderful woman named Meredith.

Did I deserve such blessings? Hardly. So why does one faithful pastor, who loves his children at least as much as I do, lose two of his kids? Why am I so bountifully blessed? What prompts something like that? Nothing but the favor of God.

♦ ♦ ♦ FAVOR AND FRIENDS ♦ ♦ ♦

Over the years, God has blessed us with many great friends. We love going out to dinner with them, and God has been pleased to advance His kingdom through our friendship. When our friends walk through challenges, we've been there for them, and they have been there for us. I must not forget my long-time friends with whom we had some meaningful moments together in seminary. It's indescribably wonderful to have quality friends who also serve God.

Why have we been able to develop such good and healthy friendships, when so many pastors I know have not? Is it because we share a few things in common? Or is something else going on here? What makes great friendships like these possible? I believe it is nothing but the favor of God.

I relate these incidents for no other reason than to illustrate the huge difference that enjoying the favor of God can make to your life. The favor of God is not for pastors alone, but also for truck drivers, school teachers, grocery clerks, engineers, professional models, fast food cooks, salespeople, factory workers, newspaper reporters, advertising executives, postal workers, and day care providers. Favor falls on men and women, boys and girls. It's for moms and dads, aunts and uncles, grandmas and grandpas. It's for single people and married people, urban people and country people. It affects Republicans and Democrats and Libertarians and independents.

> No matter who you are, where you live, or what you do for a living, you can set yourself up to receive — and be blessed out of your socks by the favor of God.
>
> ♦ ♦ ♦

♦ ♦ ♦ WHAT IS THE FAVOR OF GOD? ♦ ♦ ♦

How can favor make a difference to your life? To find the best answers to those key questions, we have to turn to the Word of God. You will be amazed at the answers you find there!

I began scouring the Bible a couple of years ago to learn all I could about the favor of God. The first thing that surprised me was how often the subject came up in both Old and New Testaments. Many crucial points in biblical history turn on whether someone did or did not receive the favor of God. If you read the Book of Genesis, you will see the favor of God popping up at the most important places and times.

Consider the very first time in the Bible that we see favor come into play:

> *In the course of time Cain brought some of the fruits of the soil as an offering to the LORD. But Abel brought fat portions from some of the firstborn of his flock. The LORD looked with favor on Abel and his offering, but on Cain and his offering he did not look with favor.*[1]

The word translated "favor" here is the Hebrew term *sa ah*, which means to gaze steadily with interest or to regard with favor. The word never refers to a casual or disinterested glance. When God grants someone His favor, He takes a keen and lively interest in that person. He observes, watches, studies, and lovingly fixes His steady gaze on the one so favored. What an amazing privilege!

So then, the favor of God is when God fixes His gaze upon you, even the details of your life.

People want to make a difference with their life. If you want your life to make a difference, change the world of business, and make your life count for eternity, you will not be able to maximize your life without finding the favor of God.

Why did God look with favor on Abel's offering, but not on Cain's? We're not explicitly told. God always wants our best, however, and God always honors wholehearted obedience. I believe God favored Abel because of two things. First, he gave God the firstborn, the best. Second, he did so with an obedient spirit. God tends to show His favor to those who eagerly obey Him.

Conversely, Cain did not choose to do right, and so presented God an unacceptable offering. He ignored God's admonition to do what was right. In the end, he committed the Bible's first murder. And so the Bible remembers Cain as someone who *"was of the evil one,"*[2] and contrasts him with his *"righteous"* brother.[3]

♦ ♦ ♦ FINDING GOD'S FAVOR ♦ ♦ ♦

When you think of Noah and the ark, what comes to mind? Perhaps you picture cute little children's books filled with cuddly animals and a quaint little boat, or an adorable, soft mobile hung over the crib of an infant. Only rarely, it seems, do most of us picture a devastated world devoid of all life except for one seasick man and his woozy family, all of whom spent almost a year bobbing on a swollen sea with a zoo full of equally seasick wild animals.

Remember the story? Humankind had grown so brutish and wicked that God was determined to wipe out the entire evil race. He decided to send a flood that would take the lives of everyone on earth — well, almost everyone. The Bible says simply, *"Noah, however, found favor in the eyes of the LORD."*[4]

The word translated "favor" in this passage is not *sa ah*, but *hen*. This is the Hebrew word most often translated "favor" in our English versions, and it means friendly regard, approval, or gracious kindness. It is used to describe any free act of kindness toward another. The word usually describes a strong personal relationship, often between a superior and a subject.

In the Bible, "to find favor" means to receive the attention and respect of another, and to receive great benefits from that person. The word often has the sense of showing kindness to the poor and needy.

> THE FAVOR OF GOD CAN ACTUALLY MAKE THE DIFFERENCE BETWEEN LIFE AND DEATH! AND NOBODY KNEW THAT BETTER THAN NOAH.
>
> ♦ ♦ ♦

Why did Noah receive God's favor? Again, we're not explicitly told, but immediately after learning that God bestowed His favor on Noah, we read that *"Noah was a righteous man, blameless among his contemporaries; Noah walked with God."*[5] Apparently, God loves to bestow His favor upon that kind of person.

God favored Noah, along with his family. They escaped the rampaging waters of the flood, while everyone else on earth — all those who did not receive God's favor — died in the violent, swirling deluge.

The Hebrew word *hen* comes from the verb *hanan*, and that little verb lives on in many of the names we hear every day. You heard it the last time you called for Hannah, or Anna, or Ann. You recall it whenever you speak the name Nancy or Anita or Annette, or John or Jean or Juan or Hans or Jan or even Ivan. Every one of those names descends directly from *hanan*, and should remind us of the wonderful favor of God.

♦ ♦ ♦ FINDING FAVOR IN THE NEW TESTAMENT ♦ ♦ ♦

The New Testament also tells us about the favor of God. At the very beginning of the Gospel of Luke, an old woman named Elizabeth finds out that she is going to have a son, even though for decades she had not born any children, and for decades already had been too old to get pregnant.

"The Lord has done this for me," the ecstatic woman declared. *"He has looked with favor in these days to take away my disgrace among the people."*[6]

The word translated "favor" here is the Greek term *epeidon*, which literally means "to fix one's gaze upon or to concern oneself with." It is very similar in meaning to the Hebrew term *sa ah* that we already considered. God fixed His eyes upon Elizabeth and granted her the desire of her heart, a son — a child who would grow up to become John the Baptist, the forerunner of Jesus.

The favor of God can accomplish jaw-dropping miracles! Could you use one? If so, then perhaps you may want to learn all you can about the favor of God.

One New Testament word gets translated "favor" about six times. That word is *charis*, as found in Luke 1:30, which describes an encounter between an angelic messenger and a young woman named Mary.

"Do not be afraid, Mary," the angel says, *"for you have found favor with God."* Mary had found such great favor, in fact, that God chose her from all the women in the world — and from all of human history — to bear the Savior of the world, Jesus Christ.

The same remarkable word describes Jesus himself as He grew up: *"And Jesus increased in wisdom and stature, and in favor with God and with people."*[7]

Would you like to enjoy that kind of favor? The kind that set Mary apart from all other women throughout all history? It also portrays the kind of favor that characterized the life and ministry of Jesus Christ. You don't need angelic or miraculous events to be favored; God can use the smallest details of your life for tremendous favor.

♦ ♦ ♦ FAVOR AND GRACE ♦ ♦ ♦

The idea really isn't so outlandish as it might seem, for that kind of favor. The word *charis* appears in the Bible more than a hundred other times in the form of "grace." In fact, "favor" and "grace" are closely related. We see this even in the Old Testament. Remember Noah?

While most English translations say that he found "favor" in the eyes of God, some say that he found "grace" in the eyes of God. So what's the difference? God offers His "favor" and "grace" to those who really want it. Do *you* want it? If we look at "secular" history (I tend to think of all history as bound up in God's overall plan!), we see innumerable examples.

WITHOUT ANY QUESTION AT ALL, THERE IS A STRONG CORRELATION AND RELATIONSHIP BETWEEN GRACE AND GOD'S FAVOR. ANY MEASURE OF GOD'S FAVOR THAT COMES TO YOU OR ME, TAKES PLACE FOR ONE REASON ALONE: THE GRACE OF GOD!

♦ ♦ ♦

In our own time, Beverly LaHaye became heartsick over the direction our country was taking morally, and so founded Concerned Women for America, the largest women's organization in the country. I dare say the efforts of CWA helped put the debate about morals and ethics on the national table for discussion. Beverly took on a difficult task and her willingness to do so was a factor in being favored by God. She was favored for a reason.

> THE FAVOR OF GOD IS BOTH MYSTERIOUS AND TANGIBLE.
>
> ♦ ♦ ♦

At least one other word also gets translated "favor" in the New Testament. *Dektos* means favor, acceptable, or welcome, and appears in passages such as 2 Corinthians 6:2: *"I tell you, now is the time of God's favor, now is the day of salvation"* (NIV). This kind of favor is offered to all, right now, regardless of heritage or background or personal history. God extends this kind of favor to *you* right now and says, "If you have never accepted my offer of salvation, now is the time. Don't delay. Don't put it off! All you must do to enjoy my favor in salvation is to accept it, free and without cost to you, right at this very moment."

In His great grace, God right now is extending His favor to you and me, inviting us to place our faith in His Son, Jesus Christ, who died for our sins and who rose again to bring us salvation. Have you experienced this side of God's favor? If not, I urge you to discover what it's all about. Let the favor of God smile upon you — and keep *you* smiling for all eternity! If you've already taken this step of faith and have started down the interstate of God's favor, I invite you to keep moving with me. Believe me, the wonders ahead are more than worth the trip!

♦ ♦ ♦ WHAT DOES FAVOR DO? ♦ ♦ ♦

What happens to those who personally experience the favor of God? What kind of benefits do they receive? How does the favor of God fill their lives with blessing after blessing?

Let me try to entice you with a few examples of what it means to find and enjoy God's favor. Then you tell me if it's worth pursuing with all your strength.

- Those who receive God's favor also receive "honor," along with the promise, *"He does not withhold the good from those who live with integrity."* [8]
- God's favor firmly establishes the work of a person's hands. [9]
- God's favor helps us endure tough times. [10]
- God's favor protects "the righteous" like a shield. [11]
- God's favor translates to great power in prayer. [12]
- God's favor turns even one's enemies into unexpected allies. [13]

Would you like to be honored by the Creator of the universe? Would you like to enjoy *all* of the good things that God wants to give you? If so, then you need to find and enjoy God's favor.

- Does your life feel a bit unsteady, a little shaky, and not very secure? If so, then you need to change all of that by finding and enjoying God's favor.
- Or are you going through some tough times? Do you feel under the rain clouds, in the middle of a downpour, or trapped in the snarling winds of a hurricane? If so, then you need the favor of God.
- Do you need protection? If so, then you need the favor of God.
- Would you like to see more of your prayers answered? If so, then you need the favor of God.
- Could you use some help from an unlikely source? If so, then you need the favor of God.

♦ ♦ ♦ The Difference Between Success and Failure ♦ ♦ ♦

Finding the favor of God can mean the difference between success and failure, joy and heartache, laughter and tears, even life and death. Neither you nor I can order God to give us the full range of His favor. We also cannot manipulate Him into a corner so that He has no choice but to grant it to us. He grants His favor according to his love and grace and not necessarily according to our achievements or personal record of godliness.

[Yet, as one Bible hero shows us, we can also align ourselves with God's purposes and God's desires that we place ourselves in a prime position to experience God's favor. That should give us great hope!]

♦ ♦ ♦ Attracting God's Favor: David ♦ ♦ ♦

The life of David shows us that while we can never "deserve" or "earn" God's favor, we can live in a way that tends to attract His favorable attention.

David began life as the youngest and least regarded son in a family of little to no national influence. In fact, David had earned so little respect by his early teen years that his father didn't even include him when the prophet Samuel — a figure of enormous national prominence — stopped by the family homestead to see all of Jesse's sons.[14] Yet despite David's apparent unimportance, God tapped him to succeed Saul as king of Israel.

Had David earned such a privilege? Clearly, not. Then why did God pick him over every other young man in Israel? Why not pick Jonathan, the son of Saul and rightful heir to the throne, who became David's closest earthly friend? Jonathan, after all, possessed many of the same godly qualities that David demonstrated. So why was David chosen and not Jonathan?

Chalk it up to the favor of God. That, at least, is the New Testament's take on the subject. In a massively politically incorrect summary of Israel's history, Stephen, the first martyr of the church, described David simply as one who "found favor in God's sight."[15]

Stephen could have used many other terms to picture the great David: king, prophet, warrior, poet, singer, conqueror of Jerusalem, ancestor of Jesus.

Stephen chose none of those terms. Instead, he summed up the life of David with a single thought: the man enjoyed God's favor.

We don't have to take Stephen's word for it, of course. Jesus himself did a pretty good job of summing up David's life and the favor he enjoyed after David declared his desire to build a permanent home for the ark of the covenant. God instructed the prophet Nathan to tell David:

> *I took you from the pasture and from following the sheep to be ruler over my people Israel. I have been with you wherever you have gone, and I have destroyed all your enemies before you. I will make a name for you like that of the greatest in the land. . . . I will give you rest from all your enemies.*
>
> *The LORD declares to you: The LORD himself will make a house for you. . . . I will raise up after you your descendant, who will come from your body, and I will establish his kingdom. He will build a house for my Name, and I will establish the throne of his kingdom forever. . . . Your house and kingdom will endure before Me forever, and your throne will be established forever.*[16]

Isn't our God amazing? He really wants to favor you!

Many centuries later, Stephen looked at the life of David and proclaimed that the king owed everything good in his life to the favor of God. Just consider how the gracious, undeserved favor of God had blessed David so tremendously:

- God took a boy who "followed" sheep and turned him into a man who "ruled" the Lord's own people.
- God went with David wherever he went, even into the hard and difficult places.
- God caused the defeat of all David's enemies and gave him rest from the battlefield.

- God, by His own choice, decided to build a "house" for David, when David had expressed a desire to build a "house" for God.

- God would make sure that David's kingdom never ended.

♦ ♦ ♦ GRACE UNMERITED ♦ ♦ ♦

What could such favor be other than God's grace being demonstrated? How would David have seen it, other than as a gracious gesture from his Almighty Lord?

Did David "earn" any of this gracious treatment? No. Did he receive this abundance of divine favor as payment in return for good deeds? No. God's favor can't be earned, nor can it be received as a wage for labor performed. David knew this — and sadly, he would see the flip side to this truth many years later.

One sad day, David committed adultery with another man's wife, and then arranged for his murder. The Lord held David fully accountable for his reprehensible actions and reminded David both of His favor and how the king had so badly abused it:

> *I anointed you king over Israel, and I delivered you from the hand of Saul. I gave your master's house to you and your master's wives into your arms, and I gave you the house of Israel and Judah, and if that was not enough, I would have given you even more.*
>
> *Why then have you despised the command of the LORD by doing what I consider evil? You struck down Uriah the Hittite with the sword and took his wife as your own wife — you murdered him with the Ammonite's sword. Now therefore, the sword will never leave your house because you despised Me and took the wife of Uriah the Hittite to be your own wife.*[17]

To my mind, the saddest line of all appears after the Lord recounts the staggering favor He had shown to David before his affair. *"And if that was not enough,"* the Lord says mournfully, *"I would have given you even more."* What amazing favor did David forfeit by his foolishness? We'll never know.

David understood that he could not demand God's favor. When the child born through his adultery fell gravely ill, and Nathan the prophet declared that the little boy would surely die, *"David pleaded with God for the boy. He fasted, went home, and spent the night lying on the ground. . . . and would not eat anything."*[18] Later, to a bewildered cadre of servants, David explained his behavior: *"While the baby was alive, I fasted and wept because I thought, 'Who knows? The LORD may be gracious to me and let him live.'"*[19]

This is the *"perhaps"* of God's favor. In this case, the "perhaps" came up a "no." The child died.

HAVE YOU EVER CONSIDERED HOW MUCH FAVOR YOU MISS WHEN YOU FAIL TO BE WHAT GOD WANTS YOU TO BE? HAVE YOU EVER WONDERED WHAT YOUR LIFE WOULD BE LIKE IF GOD SET HIS GAZE ON YOU FOR A LIFETIME?

◆ ◆ ◆

All along, David knew that he could never demand divine favor. Yet still he asked for it. How did the king respond when this time God did not show David His favor? What did David do when his infant son died? Did he curse God? Scream at Him? Accuse Him, berate Him, scorn Him, or abandon Him? No. A man who has tasted the favor of God knows there is nothing better, even when that favor eludes him for a time. Instead, the Bible says, *"Then David got up from the ground. He washed, anointed himself, changed his clothes, went to the LORD's house, and worshiped."*[20]

That's what a man who has experienced the favor of God does, even when he confesses his deep and terrible guilt. Those who have tasted God's favor can never get enough of that favor. So they pray for it, hope for it, and look for it. They do so not because they deserve it, but because they know God is gracious.

David, the Bible tells us, was a man after God's own heart.[21] Although Scripture does not say so, the reverse seems just as true to me — the Lord was a God after David's own heart. When those two things come together, I doubt God's favor can lag far behind.

It's good to get in on the open "secret" of God's good favor. It encourages our hearts to know that it exists, that it has blessed and continues to bless God's people, and that it can clear away the darkest clouds and roll back the loudest thunder.

But in another way — so what? How can knowing about God's favor benefit us right now, right here, right where we are? If that favor is an expression of God's grace and something we can't earn, work for, or deserve, then what *practical* difference can knowing about it make in our day-to-day lives?

I think the apostle Paul would like to handle that one. In telling a few friends about some rough times he endured in one far-flung corner of the world, he once let slip another little "secret" about God's gracious favor. Paul didn't merely want them to know of God's existence but, instead, he implored them to *pray for it!*

Paul told his friends that God had not only delivered him from a terrible end, but that he expected him to continue to do so in whatever adventures awaited him. He told them that on God *"we have set our hope that he will continue to deliver us."* How could Paul entertain such a hope? Where did he muster the confidence that God would continue to deliver him? It grew in his heart. Paul told his friends, *"As you help us by your prayers. Then many will give thanks on our behalf for the gracious favor granted us in answer to the prayers of many."* [22]

Yes, God's favor is a gracious gesture, free and undeserved and unearned — on the house, so to speak. By his example, Paul urges you and me to *pray for it!* This is not some creaky old theological relic to be dusted off and appraised at an antique show. Instead it is a living, dynamic, potent force for good that Paul thinks we should be calling down on one another.

It is called "favor," the favor of God; that incredible experience when God fixes His gaze upon you, even the details of your life.

So, just one last question, and I'm done.

Are we?

2

A SOVEREIGN SIGN

In the weeks that followed the successful Allied invasion of France in June 1944, hope rose that the terrible conflict could be over by Christmas. Troops prayed, parents stormed heaven, and sweethearts cried out for supernatural protection.

Hard fighting against a desperate Nazi war machine dashed those hopes. By December, American troops were dug in along the German border, ironically, in similar positions that their fathers found themselves in a generation before.

What the American and British commanders couldn't know was that Hitler had concocted one last desperate gamble to survive. Ordering several divisions into the wintry mix that surrounded spread-out American forces, Hitler hoped that he could break out and create conditions for a cease-fire. This became the basis for the famous Battle of the Bulge.

When poor weather conditions grounded Allied planes, Gen. George S. Patton "ordered" a prayer from the Third Army chaplain: "Almighty and most merciful Father, we humbly beseech Thee, of Thy great goodness, to restrain these immoderate rains with which we have had to contend. Grant us fair weather for battle. Graciously hearken to us as soldiers who call upon Thee that, armed with Thy power, we may advance from victory to victory, and crush the oppression and wickedness of our enemies and establish Thy justice among men and nations."

As everyone knows, the prayer "worked," and Patton's tanks were able to relieve trapped American soldiers in the key Belgian town of Bastogne. The Germans were repelled and, to this day, many consider this to be a sign that God's favor was with the Allied war effort, to put an end to tyranny in Europe.

Life has a way of throwing us some nasty curves, doesn't it?

♦ ♦ ♦ OUR GOD REIGNS ♦ ♦ ♦

After a dozen or so years of happy marriage, I looked at Jeana and saw a young, beautiful, 35-year-old woman with two healthy little boys. We were enjoying ministry and enjoying life.

On an average Monday morning in an average January, Jeana had a routine biopsy done on one of her breasts. "Don't worry about coming with me," she said. I accompanied her anyway.

Two hours after arriving at the doctor's office, our lives changed forever. We could tell from the doctor's facial expression that he had something other than good news to report. He did — breast cancer.

Immediately, we pursued the best medical treatment we could find. We visited an experienced oncologist and tried to make an informed decision about what kind of surgery we should choose, how extensive it should be, and how we could go about finding out if cancer had invaded any other part of her body.

All of that took a couple of anxiety-filled weeks. During that time we decided to take Jeana to one of the best cancer facilities in the world, the M.D. Anderson Hospital in Houston, Texas. And there we found ourselves, in a huge, sprawling city. As a mother, Jeana worried that she might never see her precious two little boys grow up. Both of us were scared out of our minds.

I'll never forget the day we visited the hospital for the first time. Because we had arrived a little early, we visited a Christian bookstore to spend a few minutes. As we drove up to the hospital, fearful in every way, a song from a CD I had just purchased began to ring out: "Our God Reigns." I felt as though God were saying to me, "Everything's fine, Ronnie. I'm going to take care of everything."

In that year, I had felt led by God to pray and fast for one day every week, asking that God would do something powerful for my wife. One day I sensed God giving me a word from Isaiah 43:1–3:

Now this is what the LORD says — the One who created you, O Jacob, and the One who formed you, O Israel:

*"**Do not fear**, for I have redeemed you; I have called you by your name; you are Mine.*

*I **will be with you** when you pass through the waters, and when you pass through the rivers, they will not overwhelm you.*

*You **will not be scorched** when you walk through the fire, and the flame will not burn you.*

For I am the LORD, your God, the Holy One of Israel, and your Savior.

♦ ♦ ♦ PUT THROUGH THE FIRE ♦ ♦ ♦

I believed God was telling me that He was going to put us through the fire, but that in the end, Jeana was going to be fine. With such confirmation, we walked by faith in that word.

After one major surgery, a couple of supporting surgeries, six months of chemotherapy, and six weeks of radiation treatment, doctors declared Jeana free of cancer. That was more than 15 years ago. Since then she has remained free of that terrible disease — I believe because of the favor of God.

Because of her ordeal, Jeana has had countless opportunities through the years to support other women going through uncertain times, and pointing them to the only Savior who can heal their bodies and give health and strength to their souls.

We have felt enormously grateful to God, not only for her healing, but also for the way He has allowed her to use her time of trouble for the good of thousands of women across the country.

Still, Jeana has a question. It's not, "Why did God make me go through such suffering?" Nor is it, "How could a good God allow such a horrible disease to exist?" It's not even, "What could I have done to escape such an ugly experience?"

Jeana had buried many of her friends who also suffered with cancer. The question she has asked me more than once is a question to which I have no real answer: "Why did I make it when so many others have not?" I have heard her say it this way: "Why not me?"

Even though God was busy maturing our views on what He might be up to, we both felt very anxious. Questions abounded that I voiced only to God. Would she die? How would I raise the boys if she passed away? What in the world would I do?

"Were you scared?" Yes, I was scared! I felt both fear and a calmness of faith at the same time. If I had not taken the measures I did, I'm not sure how I would have handled it.

Jeana and I both know that she didn't "deserve" to get cancer, any more than the person who lives to be 103 and yet never suffers a sick day in her life. We also know that she didn't "deserve" to get healed of the disease, any more than her friends who died of it. So why her? Why did God choose to spare her life, but not the lives of so many of her friends? Why did He show her such favor, and not others? Why?

Could it come down to prayer? I fasted and prayed, after all. Yet I know there are thousands of husbands at least as godly as me, and who love their wives at least as much I do, and who pray more fervently and more often and longer than I ever did — and yet my wife is alive and theirs are not. Why?

Ultimately, it is God who gives His favor to those He chooses, for His own reasons and for His own purposes. He doesn't need our permission. He doesn't need our counsel. He bestows His favor or withholds it, exactly as He wishes.

In other words, the favor of God is not only a gracious gesture, it's also a sovereign sign. When it flows into our lives, it comes to us as a sign or a token of His free choice. We need to remember that we serve a God who *"does what He wants with the army of heaven and the inhabitants of the earth."*[1]

♦ ♦ ♦ FAVOR: GOD'S SOVEREIGN SIGN ♦ ♦ ♦

That includes you. That includes me, and that includes Jeana, too.

I'm so very grateful to God that He showed us His favor by sparing Jeana's life and giving back her health. We know that He has a great plan for the rest of her years on earth and that He has so much more for her to do. Every bit of that wonderful news I consider an expression of His good favor — a favor that He gives to whomever He chooses, whenever and however He chooses to give it.

I don't know a better way to say it: His favor is a sovereign sign.

♦ ♦ ♦ HE DOES AS HE PLEASES ♦ ♦ ♦

God gives His favor to those He chooses, through no merit or effort of their own. While we can and should position ourselves to get in the best possible spot to attract His favorable attention, He is never under any obligation whatsoever to grant us His favor unless He obligates himself to do so.

God does what God wants to do. We cannot tie His hands or bind Him to this or that action by anything we do or say or think or pray. God is sovereign! That means He is the supreme ruler of this universe. He answers to no one. No Supreme Court can overturn His decisions and no independent power can force His hand. He is the one who is, who was, and who is to come.[2] He is the one who opens and no one will close, and closes and no one opens.[3]

> **HE IS THE SUPREME RULER OF THIS UNIVERSE AND THE ONLY ONE OF SUPER RANK. HE IS THE ONLY ONE IN COMPLETE CONTROL OF ALL THINGS. HE IS SOVEREIGN!**
>
> **♦ ♦ ♦**

♦ ♦ ♦ THE TIME OF GOD'S FAVOR ♦ ♦ ♦

That goes just as much for His favor as it does for everything else.

An interesting phrase keeps popping up in the Bible that speaks volumes about God's favor as a sovereign sign. Over and over again we read about "the time of God's favor."

- **Psalm 69:13** — *"But as for me, LORD, my prayer to You is for a time of favor. In Your abundant, faithful love, God, answer me with Your sure salvation."* When life makes no sense to us, we pray that *this*, at last, will be the time of God's favor upon us. We pray that in His sovereign pleasure, He will shower us with His favor.

- **Psalm 102:13** — *"You will arise and have compassion on Zion, for it is time to show favor to her — the appointed time has come."* At times and seasons on God's sovereign calendar, He acts toward us in His good favor — and He appoints those times for His own purposes and His own reasons.

- **Isaiah 49:8** — *"This is what the LORD says: 'In the time of my favor I will answer you, and in the day of salvation I will help you'"* (NIV). God shows us His favor in what He calls, "the time of my favor." He chooses that time in His sovereign wisdom.

- **Isaiah 61:1–2** — *"The Spirit of the Lord GOD is on Me, because the LORD has anointed Me to bring good news to the poor. He has sent Me to heal the brokenhearted, to proclaim liberty to the captives, and freedom to the prisoners; to proclaim the year of the LORD's favor."*

◆ ◆ ◆ A TIME FOR GOD'S FAVOR ◆ ◆ ◆

Jesus quoted and appropriated Isaiah 61:1-2 for himself in Luke 4:18–19. In doing so, He was declaring that His arrival signaled the time of God's favor for Israel. The long-prophesied Messiah had finally arrived to fulfill God's gracious promise, at exactly the right time: *"But when the completion of the time came, God sent His Son, born of a woman, born under the law, to redeem those under the law, so that we might receive adoption as sons."*[4]

There is a "time of God's favor," and our Lord chooses those times in His sovereign pleasure. Does that encourage you? Quite honestly, sometimes that appears to be great news and, at other times, it doesn't. In order to have positive approach to the sovereignty of God we must continually ask ourselves, "What does God appear to be doing?"

The fact is, when most of us start reading Bible passages that speak of the sovereign will of God, we tend to get uncomfortable. That includes preachers!

I will never forget what author and pastor John McArthur once told me. I was struggling with the implications of divine sovereignty, and he said to me, "You know, Ronnie, you just need to preach the Word of God. When you come across the sovereignty of God in a text, you just preach it like that's all you believe. When you come across the free will of man in another Bible passage, you preach it the same way, like that's all you believe. You just have to trust God to bring balance to your people."

Why does God give His sovereign favor to people? First, to build His kingdom. Now read very carefully. How many resources do you have? Look at your bank account. Look at your stock market. Look at your property. Whatever you have in resources, whatever you have in giftedness . . . what is your giftedness? "I'm not sure I have a gift." No, you have gifts. If you're saved, you have gifts. Whatever you have in giftedness, God has given you sovereign favor over those things to do what? To build the kingdom of God. That's exactly what He did with David. That's exactly what He did with Solomon. It doesn't make sense sometimes, but He does it.

God's purpose, God's purpose for you, is much greater than building a company, business, team, career, or even a family. God's purpose is greater than all those things. Is there anything wrong with building a company? No. Anything wrong with building a business? No. A team? No. A career? No. A family? Absolutely not. Your purpose in life is much, much, much greater than all those things. To be quite honest, I am not sure that a lot of us believe the statement that you see today. So what is it? God is always moving in a sovereign way to do one thing. You know what it is? Build His kingdom. He is very committed to building His kingdom.

Let me give you an illustration of this. During one of our church's recent mission trips to China, our group was contacted by a man named Mr. Wong. That's not his real name, but for security reasons I have to give you this made-up name, Mr. Wong. He is a Ph.D. professor in a major university in China. He is a registered Christian and shares Christ with his students actively.

Due to his courage in sharing Christ, he was demoted recently in the university and was threatened with a prison sentence for his faith. Mr. Wong needed encouragement.

Our mission team met with him, prayed for him, and gave him a treasured copy of the New Testament and some other materials which he clutched to his chest the moment he received them.

Mr. Wong shared with our group about a married couple that had come to America to study. He said the last thing this couple did before coming to America was invite Mr. Wong to dinner. This couple told Mr. Wong that his witnessing for Christ was nonsense and was hurting his family and his career. They told him he needed to cease talking about Christ and they were not interested in hearing about Mr. Wong's Jesus.

This married couple came to America. They attended a university, the University of Arkansas. The couple began to attend a Bible study, then a church; initially the Church at Pinnacle Hills and then the First Baptist Church of Springdale, so they could hear the sermon in the Mandarin language which Mona Ross translates via closed-circuit headsets each week. After a few months of hearing the gospel, this married couple from China, who had told Mr. Wong that his faith was nonsense and they were not interested in his Jesus, *both professed Christ.* Shortly after this, they were baptized. They are now active members in our church, and the reason Mr. Wong knew our mission team was coming to his city was that this couple called to tell Mr. Wong of their decision to follow Jesus and they thanked him for sharing Jesus Christ with them. Some of us may say, "Well, what a small world." Let me tell you what I have to say about that:

What a big, sovereign God!

That is a God who is committed to building His kingdom.

It reminds me of what King David declared, however. *"Our God is in heaven and does whatever He pleases,"* in Psalm 115:3. You know one of the things that pleases God? Building His kingdom, ladies and gentlemen. I promise you today, if it could just click into our lives, and into our hearts, and into our brains today that God's intention for your life is much greater than building your life and your career and your family and your stuff. Your life cannot be maximized in anyway whatsoever apart from experiencing the favor of God. You're the one losing. And when you lose, the Kingdom does not become all that God wants it to become by using your life.

But God does not only do it to build His kingdom. Here's the second reason God demonstrates His sovereign favor to people — also to build you. He does it to build you. God wants to build you. What does He want to build you for? While we are on this earth, maybe we don't say it with our words because we don't want to be misunderstood. Some of us may be foolish enough to say it with our words, when we say, "I am in charge," "I want to do this," "I have this dream," "I'm going to get this done," "I'm going to do it my way." While we're here doing that on this earth, you know what God is saying? Our sovereign God is telling us these things, and He's always showing these truths. He is saying, "I am in charge. I have a better plan for you. I see the end from the beginning and I will always do it My way." Therefore, when you understand this about the sovereign God, you learn that each event, each experience, every person you meet, every crisis you go through, every disappointment you face, every illness that you go through, every loss that you experience in your life, and even every blessing that God gives to you, is not only for the purpose of building the kingdom, but it's also there to build you. To build you what? Well, let's look at that.

The Bible tells us in the Book of Romans. Notice what God's Word says in 8:28: *"We know that all things work together for the good of those who love God:"* — do you believe that today? — *"those who are called according to His purpose. For those He foreknew He also predestined"* — notice this key statement — *"to be conformed to the image of His Son, so He would*

> GOD IS COMMITTED 100 PERCENT TO MAKE YOU MORE LIKE HIS SON, JESUS CHRIST. AND HE WILL DO WHATEVER HE HAS TO DO TO GET YOU TO THAT POINT.
>
> ◆ ◆ ◆

be the firstborn among many brothers. And those He predestined, He also called; and those He called, He also justified; and those He justified, He also glorified."

It is God's intention to build you into the likeness of Christ, and He uses every experience to do that, each event to do that, each disappointment to do that, each illness to do that, each loss you face to do that. I'm telling you, our God is committed 100 percent to make you more like His Son, Jesus Christ. He will do whatever He has to do to get you to that point. Sometimes those schools are not easy. That is one seminary that is not fun to attend. But God is committed to do it. "Why has what happened to me happened *to me?*" you might ask. Very simple. God wants to use all of that to build His kingdom. God wants to use all of that to build you into the likeness of His Son, Jesus Christ.

◆ ◆ ◆ WILL MY DREAMS COME TRUE? ◆ ◆ ◆

Maybe a short illustration would help to show how we can balance the truth of God's sovereignty with the equal truth of our ability to choose. The topic of personal dreams may provide a fertile plot for our discussion.

God often puts dreams that need to be pursued in a believer's heart, but many of us make a big mistake. We think that just because we have a particular dream — even one we're sure is from God — that he will cause it to unfold just as we think he should. But it doesn't always turn out that way.

◆ ◆ ◆ KING DAVID'S PASSION ◆ ◆ ◆

The best biblical example I know of is King David. David expressed a passionate desire to build the temple in Jerusalem. He had a dream to construct a "house" to give shelter to the ark of the covenant, where God said He would make His special presence known. This was his cherished dream. When he told the prophet Nathan about it, Nathan replied, *"Go and do all that is on your heart, for the LORD is with you."*[5]

But you know what? God didn't let David build the temple. The very next day the Lord sent Nathan back to David with some unexpected news. God told David, *"You did well to have this desire. Yet you are not the one to build it; instead, your son, your own offspring, will build it for My name."*[6]

Was David's dream from God? It seems so, for God told him that he "did well" to have this dream in his heart. His dream was a good thing, and "good" is practically God's middle name. Nevertheless, God did not allow that dream to take shape as David had envisioned it. How could this be?

I believe that dream did come from God. I think God used the king's good dream to bring David along spiritually in many areas. God did not will that David's good dream should come true. In other words, while it was God's sovereign will for David to dream the dream, it was also God's sovereign will that the dream go unfulfilled. God wanted to use the king's dream to help David mature spiritually, but He did not allow David to confuse his good dream with God's good and sovereign will. The two are not necessarily the same thing.

I wonder if a lot of us don't struggle with this issue. We have become so used to thinking of ourselves as the center of the universe, that it shocks us to see that we really aren't. God's sovereignty reminds us that it's really all about Him, not about us. Regardless of what our current culture tells us, God does what He desires, when He desires, how He desires, for whom He desires.

Up until this time, it has been God's plan for our ministry to build in northwest Arkansas, not Houston or Los Angeles or Chicago or any other major metropolitan city. I can be puzzled by this, or not, but at the end of the day, God does as He wills.

David recognized that God rules absolutely as the sovereign of the universe. When the Lord told the king that he could not build the temple, David responded with a long prayer of praise and thanksgiving. Tellingly, no fewer than five times he called his God, "Sovereign LORD" (NIV).[7] David embraced the truth proclaimed in passages like Psalm 115:3: *"Our God is in heaven and does whatever He pleases"* — and Psalm 135:6: *"The LORD does whatever He pleases in heaven and on earth, in the seas and all the depths."* David understood, accepted, and embraced the facts:

- **God does what God wants to do**. As Isaiah says, *"The LORD of Hosts Himself has planned it; therefore, who can stand in its way?"*[8]

- **God has a plan that He fulfills through exercising His sovereignty**. As the Psalmist tells us, *"The LORD frustrates the counsel of the nations; He thwarts the plans of the peoples. The counsel of the LORD stands forever, the plans of His heart from generation to generation."*[9]

- **God matures us in Christ through what He brings into our lives.** Whatever God does in us and through us, He does so that we may grow *"with growth from God."*[10]

Have you come to grips with this bedrock truth about God's sovereignty?

What dreams is God nurturing in your heart right now? What have you chosen to do with those dreams? Are you willing to pursue them as far as God sovereignly leads? Do so now and trust God in His wisdom and love.

◆ ◆ ◆ GOD IN CHARGE ◆ ◆ ◆

Everywhere in the biblical Book of Daniel, we see God totally in charge, showing His favor to those who have well positioned themselves to receive it.

That's why I think it might surprise you to see how Daniel responds to God's sovereignty once you get to chapter 9. There we learn that, as he read from the Book of Jeremiah, Daniel understood that God had ordained for the people of Israel to remain in Babylonian captivity for 70 years — no more, no less. So what does Daniel do, this favored man who witnessed and experienced and understood divine sovereignty like almost no one else? Daniel starts praying that God would release His people from captivity after the 70 years conclude!

Our Western minds tend to think, *Why bother? God said He's going to do it, so why pray about it?* Daniel reads the same text we do, however, and it gives him powerful motivation to pray with confidence. This makes me wonder if he understood something about prayer that many of us do not.

In his praying, Daniel confesses that, *"We have not sought the favor of the LORD our God by turning from our sins and giving attention to your truth."*[11] He considered it a sin that his people had not sought God's favor! So what does he do? He prays, *"Therefore, our God, hear the prayer and the petitions of Your servant. Show Your favor to Your desolate sanctuary for the Lord's sake."*[12]

Daniel had received God's favor his whole life, but he wanted that favor to extend to his whole nation. What did he do? He prayed for it. By his godly example, he showed everyone who watched how to set themselves up to receive the favor of God.

Do you want to set yourself up to receive God's favor? Then learn from Daniel.

- **By faith, turn from your sins** and give attention to God's truth in the Bible.
- **Pray for God's favor**. Yes, Daniel tells us, God is indeed sovereign — but if you want to experience His favor, you can do something to give yourself the best chance of receiving it.

♦ ♦ ♦ GETTING IN POSITION ♦ ♦ ♦

God bestows His favor on those He chooses, when He chooses, and how He chooses. "But why should I do anything regarding His favor,

WHAT ARE YOU LEARNING RIGHT NOW ABOUT WHAT GOD SEEMS TO BE DOING IN YOUR LIFE? WHAT ARE YOU LEARNING ABOUT GOD? ABOUT HIS ACTIVITY? ABOUT YOURSELF?

♦ ♦ ♦

then," someone objects, "when He's going to do what He's going to do?"

Daniel shows us that we are much more likely to receive God's sovereign favor if we position ourselves correctly. In his terms, we should seek God's favor by turning from our sins and giving attention to His truth.

Is there a mystery here? You bet! I began to understand part of that mystery just weeks after Jeana's cancer diagnosis. Manley Beasley, a respected revivalist, who is now with the Lord, called us and said, "This is not about whether you die or not, but it is about you getting out of this experience all God wants you to get."

He spoke from firsthand experience, having endured countless physical challenges through the years. He taught us that part of the mystery of where God's favor and God's sovereignty overlap can be explained by what He wants to produce in our lives. But not all of it!

The better part of the mystery remains. Therefore, I think it might help to try to shine a little light on that very dark corner. Let's take a journey now into the heart of a great mystery.

FINDING THE FAVOR OF GOD

A
MYSTERIOUS
MANIFESTATION

3

I grew up in a small church located in the simple southwest Texas town of Yoakum. I doubt the population ever grew to more than about 5,500 residents, and the church never attracted more than about 40 parishioners to its regular Sunday services. When I left town, I didn't know that any church service, anywhere, ever enticed more than a couple of hundred people to show up.

I went to college by faith. I sure didn't have the funds for it, but the Lord provided, taking care of all my needs and supplying me with a good education. Summer ministry jobs allowed me to save enough for the school year, and during my last year and a half, I pastored a small local church. After Jeana and I got married, she also worked at a bank.

I still remember my freshman year, as late spring began to give way to summer. I was trying to figure out, "What on earth am I going to do this summer for God?" I poked around looking for a temporary job, but in those days, few opportunities presented themselves. As I prayed through the issue, one day I felt God giving me a personal word from Psalm 75:6–7. It's been my life verse ever since:

"For promotion cometh neither from the east, nor from the west, nor from the south. But God is the judge: he putteth down one, and setteth up another" (KJV).

That summer I made a commitment that I've kept ever since: Only the Lord promotes me. I am not interested in any other kind of promotion, or one that feeds my ego or tries to build something personally for me. I learned a long time ago that when the Lord promotes you, His favor travels along as a delightful companion. I believe one of the secrets to experiencing the favor of God is yielding to the sovereignty of God and doing exactly what God calls you to do, adjusting your life according to the gift mix you have, so that you may glorify Him. It still floors me to think that I pastor a church that touches 15,000 lives. Why does God do that? I don't know.

On the other hand, because of my great zeal for evangelism and reaching the masses for Christ, I've also wondered why the Lord did not place me in a major metropolitan region of the country. I love northwest Arkansas, but it's not exactly New York or Los Angeles or even Houston. Yet every time I think we've topped out here in Arkansas, God seems to take us to a different level. It just amazes me.

All of that is nothing but the favor of God.

Several years ago I started to pray that, despite the absence of the masses, God would give me an opportunity to speak to them anyway. And amazingly, I've seen even that occur. It's happened through my books, and it's happened through unexpected media opportunities.

Our television ministry, now carried by the WGN superstation, gets beamed into homes all across North America. I've been asked to speak at various events across the country, in all kinds of formats, and for all kinds of denominations. I even had the privilege to speak to 1.4 million men at a big Promise Keepers event in Washington, D.C., back in 1997. Over the years, I've seen the Lord give me ministry opportunities that I simply never could have imagined.

Please don't think I'm bragging! Honestly, it feels a lot more like startled astonishment. It really is hard for me to believe. All of this has happened, even though I didn't know anybody.

May I be frank? The unfortunate truth is that some of national Christian ministry amounts to little more than a game. Too often it boils down to who you know and what kind of recommendation you can get from some well-known personality. It can become so silly and childish (and much of it is carnal — but let's not dwell on that). I still don't know a lot of the "big names," and yet God has given me exactly the kinds of opportunities I began praying for so many years ago. In all of this, God has shown me astonishing favor. From a human perspective, it seems to make no sense at all. It often makes me scratch my head. His favor can be so . . . well, *mysterious*.

> I DO KNOW THAT MANY PEOPLE CAN COMMUNICATE BETTER THAN ME, TEACH BETTER THAN ME, LEAD BETTER THAN ME, AND ARE JUST BETTER THAN ME. BUT FOR SOME REASON, GOD HAS TURNED HIS FAVOR TOWARD MY CAREER.
>
> ♦ ♦ ♦

♦ ♦ ♦ IT'S A MYSTERY TO ME ♦ ♦ ♦

The secular world still uses the old phrase, "God works in mysterious ways" — and, most of the time, the ones using it have no idea what they're talking about. For one thing, they tend to blame God for many horrible things in which He had no hand at all. Even in the silliness of the phrase, there remains an echo of truth.

The apostle Paul uses the Greek term *mysterion* at least 20 times in the New Testament. Often he employs it to talk about the mystery side of God. He uses the word in different ways, but usually to refer to something long-hidden that God has chosen finally to reveal. In general, the term describes the secret thoughts and plans of God, suddenly made plain to those chosen to receive the revelation. To get a feel for a biblical "mystery," consider just a few of the passages where Paul uses the term.

- **The way God moves in the heart of people is a mystery.** *"I do not want you to be ignorant of this mystery, brothers, so that you may not be conceited: Israel has experienced a hardening in part until the full number of the Gentiles has come in."* [1] *"Listen, I am telling you* *a mystery: We will not all fall asleep, but we will all be changed, in a moment, in the twinkling of an eye, at the last trumpet. For the trumpet will sound, and the dead will be raised incorruptible, and we will be changed.*"[2] Many of God's unveiled mysteries still remain shrouded in questions. When will this amazing event happen? How will it happen? We just don't know.

- **God loves to surprise, even confounding things!** *"By reading this you are able to understand my insight about the mystery of the Messiah. This was not made known to people in other generations as it is now revealed to His holy apostles and prophets by the Spirit: the Gentiles are co-heirs, members of the same body, and partners of the promise in Christ Jesus through the gospel."*[3]

- **Who in ancient Israel could ever have guessed that such a thing might happen?** *"God wanted to make known to those among the Gentiles the glorious wealth of this mystery, which is Christ in you, the hope of glory."*[4] The greatest mystery of all is that God chooses to live within us, providing us hope for the future and confidence on this mysterious journey we've begun.

- **When God reveals some of His mysteries,** the exact nature and how they "work" continues to perplex and even baffle us. We serve a very mysterious God! *"This mystery is profound. . . ."*[5]

- **It remains a mystery, for example,** why God places us where He does, while others who seem better qualified get placed somewhere else. We can't understand it. We cannot grasp God's purpose. When God seems to put down, He may be setting up; and when God seems to be setting up, He might be putting down. Jesus spoke of this phenomenon when He told us, *"But many who are first will be last, and the last first."*[6]

◆ ◆ ◆ COLLECTING MY THOUGHTS ◆ ◆ ◆

The day I started collecting my thoughts for this chapter, I called one of our senior adult women to talk to her about her very ill husband.

"You know, Pastor," she said, "I don't question God. I am entrusting him to the Lord." Within days, her husband died and entered heaven.

I think Scripture permits us to question God, but it also lets us know that, many times, we shouldn't expect to receive the answers we say we want.

Remember Peter's encounter with Jesus on the beach, after the Resurrection? The Lord had just told Peter that one day he would die for his faith in a very unpleasant way. A shaken Peter looked around, saw John, and asked, *"Lord — what about him?"* Jesus answered with a curt, *"If I want him to remain until I return, what is that to you? As for you, follow Me."*[7]

So how did things eventually turn out? Tradition tells us that while Peter died upside-down on a Roman cross, the apostle John died of old age. Why the difference? We just don't know.

A lot of what happens in life is just like that. It's plain mysterious. God seldom chooses to reveal why He does what He does. Why does He bless one man with His favor, and not another? Most of the time, the answer remains a mystery.

♦ ♦ ♦ Reasons for Mysteries ♦ ♦ ♦

I can think of two primary reasons why God often chooses to leave us in the dark about how He doles out His favor. See if you think I hit anywhere close to the mark.

1. Some things are mysteries because they're way beyond our limited understanding.

As very limited human beings, we simply don't have the capacity to comprehend a huge number of things that our infinite God does.

That's why He says through Isaiah, *"For as heaven is higher than earth, so My ways are higher than your ways, and My thoughts than your thoughts."*[8] Many times we can't understand what He's up to because His ways and methods are impossibly far beyond us.

It's as if God is a supercomputer processing a minimum of 120 bazillion gazillion quadrillion bytes of information per hundredth of a nanosecond, while we're plodding along with a hand-carved, bone abacus that's missing most of its beads. We just can't "get it." We simply don't have the required mental capacity.

Imagine that you lived in a two-dimensional world, like on the surface of a soap bubble. Your body has height and width, but no depth, and you're literally flatter than a pancake. Now suppose a superior, three-dimensional being from outside your two-dimensional world wanted to communicate with you. He wanted to let you know that something (and Someone) outside of your experience knew about your circumstances and felt deeply concerned with your welfare. Imagine that he decided to make himself known to you for the first time by taking his three-dimensional finger and poking it right next to you through the soap bubble (somehow without breaking it and thus sending you into limbo).

What would you see? When he poked his three-dimensional finger through the bubble, would you somehow recognize it for what it really was? No, you wouldn't. Remember, you're still living in two dimensions; you have zero idea of "depth" and zero way to picture it. It's just completely outside of your experience. When the superior being pokes his finger through your bubble, you see only a little dot that gets bigger as he pushes his finger in, and then gets smaller again as he pulls it out, until it disappears completely. You still have no idea about depth or a third dimension; certainly you know *something* is up, but you'll be scratching your head for some time, trying to figure out what it might be. The idea of depth still lays way beyond you, far beyond your grasp. You just don't have the capacity to understand.

> SOME THINGS GOD DOES WILL REMAIN MYSTERIES TO US FOREVER, BECAUSE WE JUST DON'T HAVE THE BRAINPOWER OR THE EXPERIENCE TO COMPREHEND HIS ACTIONS. WE LACK AN ADEQUATE FRAME OF REFERENCE TO ENABLE US TO UNDERSTAND WHAT HE'S UP TO.
>
> ◆ ◆ ◆

(If the superior being didn't later graciously use his vastly superior intellect to help clear up your confusion, perhaps you'd write a book titled, *This Bubble Is All There Is*, followed up by *Those Mysterious Circles: Why They Prove God Can't Exist*.)

Just as He says, His ways are as far above our ways as the heavens are above the earth. That's just the way it is.

♦ ♦ ♦ THE PLACE TO BE? ♦ ♦ ♦

I will never forget an event that took place as I neared graduation from Southwestern Baptist Theological Seminary. A mission church in one of the fastest growing regions of Houston, Texas, asked me to come and be voted on to be their next pastor. I enthusiastically accepted the invitation. I had always wanted to pastor a church in a major city, and this church served a brand-new community. It was *the* place to be in that part of Houston. I felt that God could call me there for life.

After I preached there, however, I learned on the ride back to the airport that I had to receive an affirmative vote from 95 percent of the members — an extremely high total. I began to wonder what might occur.

Exactly one week later, I received a call from the chairman of the pastor search committee. He seemed very distraught to have to give me the bad news: I did not receive enough votes, and the church would not extend a call to me. I felt shocked and devastated.

To be frank, I went through two or three months of absolute emotional desolation. I did not understand what had happened, nor did I think that what had happened was fair. All of my hopes and dreams seemed burned to ashes.

Many years later, as God began to allow me to experience some unusual church and ministry blessings, I went to see how that church was growing. It shocked me to learn that the church's growth had been very limited. I was amazed.

That incident helped me to understand a little more about the sovereignty of God. In my zeal to pastor that church, I had not seen what God sees. By sending me away from that position, He was protecting me, caring for me, and loving me. God protects us when we don't even know that we need to be protected!

1. What mystifies us is no mystery to God. It is simply a part of the bigger picture and the better plan for how He and His kingdom can receive the ultimate glory — and not us. Thank God that He protects me when I don't know how to protect myself!

2. Some things are mysteries because God actively hides their meaning from us. Proverbs 25:2 tells us, *"It is the glory of God to conceal a matter."* Isaiah 45:15 declares, *"Yes, you are a God who hides Himself."* The Psalmist describes the *"clouds and thick darkness"*[9] that surround our Lord, while Moses proclaims, *"The hidden things belong to the LORD our God."*[10]

3. For reasons He seldom reveals, God keeps us in the dark. We might be able to understand the secrets if He would share them, but He doesn't. So they remain mysteries to us.

In Elisha's day, a woman overwhelmed with grief due to her son's sudden death tried to approach the prophet, her old friend, for help. Gehazi, who was Elisha's servant, misunderstood her intentions and tried to push her away. But Elisha told Gehazi, *"Leave her alone — she is in severe anguish, and the LORD has hidden it from me. He hasn't told me."*[11]

Why did the Lord hide the woman's tragedy from Elisha? After all, it was through the ministry of Elisha that this formerly childless woman and her husband were able to conceive and have a son. Yet the Lord hid the problem from the great Elisha. Why? We're never told.

These are mysteries, not so much because we *can't* understand them, but because God doesn't *let* us understand them. They're His secrets. He hides them from us.

Sometimes He hides even himself. So the Psalmist asks, *"LORD, why do You stand so far away? Why do You hide in times of trouble?"*[12] And so Job agonizes, *"Why do You hide Your face and consider me Your enemy?"*[13]

As I said before, Scripture permits us to ask tough questions like these last two. But make sure you notice something else, too: God didn't answer either one.

♦ ♦ ♦ Enjoy the Fun ♦ ♦ ♦

On this side of heaven, the mystery of God's favor — who receives it and who doesn't — will forever remain with us. We can't know the full reasons why He shows His favor to one person and not to another. Often, we don't know any of the reasons at all. We remain in the dark. We can't see where we're going.

Here is my question: Why would we *want* to know, ahead of time, the whole itinerary of our journey? Why would we want to see how it all ends? To me, that takes all the fun out of it!

I've already experienced enough of the favor of God to know that "fun" is one of its best features. It's not as though I'm totally in the dark about everything in my life between now and heaven. After all, I know where I'm ultimately going to land — in a kingdom of

> I THOROUGHLY ENJOY GETTING SURPRISED BY GOD'S FAVOR.
>
> ♦ ♦ ♦

light, a place called heaven, overflowing with delight, splendor, and eternal life. I just don't know how I'm going to get there!

To me, that's a good thing. It is intriguing. That's a fun thing. In fact, a big part of the fun lies in the unfolding of the story.

♦ ♦ ♦ Taking Risks for God ♦ ♦ ♦

Do you like to take risks for God? Men and women of faith usually do. In the Old Testament, some of David's best fighters once risked their lives to get their leader a drink from a well in Bethlehem, that was occupied by enemy forces. Why would they do such a risky thing? They did it because it can feel awfully good to take risks for a person you respect and love.[14]

The New Testament, too, mentions both men and women who risked their lives for the name of our Lord Jesus Christ.[15] Paul and Barnabas, Priscilla and Aquila, Epaphroditus — they all put their lives on the line in service to the King. Service like that entails no small amount of fear, but I guarantee you this: there's some real fun in it, too! How much fun would there be if we knew for sure how everything would turn out?

You may think I'm crazy, but most of the time I really like the excitement of not knowing ahead of time whether God will show me His favor on this project or in that circumstance. I consider it fun to take the journey as it comes, waiting to see what new thing God may do around the next bend. For that reason, I really like something Paul says: *"No eye has seen and no ear has heard, And what has never come into a man's heart, Is what God has prepared For those who love Him."* [16] But how much *fun* it is to see it all unfold!

♦ ♦ ♦ A SURPRISE (OR TWO) FOR RUTH ♦ ♦ ♦

God loves to surprise us with His favor. If you don't believe that, then I suggest you re-read the brief story of Ruth in the Old Testament.

Ruth grew up as a pagan in a land not far from ancient Israel. She married into a Hebrew family, but soon her husband died, leaving her a childless widow — a terrible misfortune anytime, but especially in those days. Her mother-in-law, Naomi, urged Ruth to stay in her homeland, but Ruth insisted on accompanying her dead husband's mother back to Israel. Although she had no way to provide for herself, no family there, and no good prospects of anything, she took the opportunity.

God, however, loves to surprise men and women of faith with His favor! In Ruth's case, that meant winning the favor of a wealthy, older bachelor named Boaz. Ruth didn't know it, but Boaz and Naomi were close family relatives. He heard how she had remained faithful to Naomi in exceptionally tough circumstances, and he went out of his way to repay her for her unexpected kindness.

Ruth couldn't help but notice the special treatment he gave her, and in wonder she asked her benefactor, *"Why have I found such favor in your eyes that you notice me — a foreigner?"* [17]

In the end, Boaz marries Ruth, and soon the unlikely couple have a son, a little boy named Obed. It's a great love story. More important for us is the fact that Ruth is a young destitute widow and foreigner living far from her homeland who worships a God she met through Naomi. As a result she becomes a direct ancestor of Jesus Christ, the Son of God and

Savior of the world. Among a sea of other more likely candidates to stand in the royal lineage of Jesus, her name stands, forever enshrined in Matthew 1:5.

How's that for a great, unexpected, mysterious example of God's favor?

♦ ♦ ♦ A JOURNEY INTO MYSTERY ♦ ♦ ♦

I'd like to encourage you to walk with me down this sometimes shadowy path to God's favor, even as Ruth did. Much of it, of course, will remain dark and mysterious until God chooses to reveal it. Even in the mystery, you can pick up some valuable treasures to assist you on your way.

1. You will gain wisdom.

As you watch what God does and ponder His activity in your life, you will likely see patterns take shape that give you insight into how to enjoy more success and experience less frustration. In other words, you will increasingly gain wisdom that you can quickly put to good use.

The Book of Proverbs is often called "wisdom literature." While it should not be considered a collection of divine promises, it does tell us how life usually works out. If we do "A," then "B" usually results. If we do "C," then "D" is the typical consequence. The wiser we become, the more we begin to observe and live by these patterns.

God's favor tends to fall on those who live according to God's revealed wisdom. God's favor operates something like the Proverbs themselves. While we have no guarantee that if we do "A," then "B" will result, we discover that "B" most often results when we do "A." We are wise to pay close attention!

Remember the senior adult lady I had called to talk about her ailing husband? She told me, "So long as there is one chance of breath, we were trusting in the God of heaven to bring about the miraculous to heal my husband. He was healed, just not this side of heaven." Because she had seen God work powerfully before, she now had the faith to believe. Their situation fell into the "perhaps" of God's favor.

2. You will increase your faith.

By continuing to walk faithfully with God on this journey of mystery, our faith grows over time. We see God working in powerful ways we did not expect. Not knowing builds our trust in Him for the part of our journey that seems most dark. Not every day is bright and sunny, with miles and miles of good visibility! Much of the time, life looks cloudy to partly cloudy, and we need a burning faith to make it safely home.

It often helps our faith to grow when we experience God's unexpected favor, but our faith does not have to shrivel just because God may not do something we want Him to do. Whether God has shown you as much favor as you desire is not the issue. Learn from the favor He's already shown you, to help you walk by faith through life, even knowing that you will not understand everything God is doing. Realize that God is fulfilling His purpose in you and is building His kingdom through the process. Do that, and your faith will grow.

3. You will learn the necessity of perseverance.

I don't need to tell you that much of the journey of faith can be hard. We face opposition of various kinds, difficulties of various stripes, obstacles of various size, and hardships of various intensity. That's why the writer to the Hebrews declares, *"For you need endurance, so that after you have done God's will, you may receive what was promised."* [18]

Endurance . . . perseverance . . . stamina . . . patience . . . resolve . . . determination — God uses this journey into mystery to build all these priceless attributes into our character. And in that very process, He grants us His favor. For as James says, *"But endurance must do its complete work, so that you may be mature and complete, lacking nothing."* [19] Ponder his words: "lacking *nothing*." What is that, but the gracious, mysterious favor of God?

Are you ready to discover more of this mystery? Then let's go on a treasure hunt for divine mysteries surrounding the favor of God. I think I can confidently say that, if you stick with me on this journey into mystery, at some point along the way you're going to receive an *unbelievable* prize.

♦ ♦ ♦ Trusting in the Dark ♦ ♦ ♦

You will not understand everything that goes on in your life. Sometimes you may have an inkling why God has (or hasn't) shown you His favor, and at other times, you won't have a clue. I like to think of life as a building with curb appeal so deeply attractive and mysterious that it draws me inside to explore its many secrets. Once I enter the building, the mysteries grow deeper and richer and more exciting. The more time I spend inside, the more I see that that its Designer built it not to expose all its mysteries at once, but only a little bit at a time. I never know what's around the next corner. I can't imagine what's waiting in the next room. My time in the house of mystery fills me with all kinds of emotions, from joy to fear to wonder to sorrow to surprise to delight. But mostly, it's *fun!* I wouldn't trade this adventure for anything.

To make a success of it, however — to wind up where I really want to be — I have to trust that God is at work. I have to believe that everything is okay. Just because I don't understand what happens in this or that room, doesn't mean I've lost His favor.

God's Word is good even when it doesn't seem to make sense. I do believe this type of wisdom has to come with spiritual maturity. The longer I live, walking with God daily, the more calm I am in the face of unusual circumstances.

Ah, but there's the mystery! As I said, I wouldn't trade it for the world. And if you're smart, you won't, either.

PART TWO

FINDING GOD'S FAVOR

It's one thing to know what God's favor is; it's quite another to spot it in your own life. Have you ever wondered where God's favor might already rest on you? No doubt, His hand of favor has touched you and shaped you and molded and blessed you in ways you might not even have recognized. This section will help you to embark on a personal investigation aimed at identifying the favor of God in your life — this gracious, sovereign, and mysterious blessing of heaven.

FINDING THE FAVOR OF GOD

SEEKING GOD'S FAVOR

4

Gene Layman gets up every morning, drives to a local fast food restaurant, and there seeks God.

He takes his Bible and drinks coffee and talks to God and reads from the Scriptures. He feels a great compulsion to seek God, to seek His will, to seek God's thumbprint on his life, and to seek His favor.

I've known Gene for a long time. He was the primary human force behind calling me to pastor the First Baptist Church of Springdale almost two decades ago. Over the years, he has served in various ministry positions in our church, but the one he cherishes the most is serving as "spiritual counselor" to the worship ministry. Back when I used to teach a pastor's class, he also worked with me to get the class ready to hear from God. He'd take the first ten minutes to set a devotional tone, speaking about what God had just shown him. He never recounted old stories or ancient history; it was always what God had shown him just that week.

Gene is a godly man who chronically reads the Word of God. As a result he has earned a reputation as a strong prayer warrior. He has developed a tremendous heart to touch the world for Christ and feels driven to ministry across the planet. He has a tremendous servant's heart.

Gene is not a pastor, and never has been. Today he's semi-retired, although for most of his years he was a hard-working businessman who owned a furniture store. For all the time I've known him, God has shown Gene great favor in his business, in his personal life, and in his church life.

I have to believe that one of the great reasons for this is that Gene asked for it. He asked and kept on asking that God might show him His favor. And God has been delighted to oblige him.

♦ ♦ ♦ IT'S OKAY TO ASK ♦ ♦ ♦

I t's okay to seek God's favor. It really is! We tend to think, *Oh, I shouldn't ask God for too much*, or *God already knows my need*. But the Bible tells us: *"Keep asking, and it will be given to you. Keep searching, and you will find. Keep knocking, and the door will be opened to you."*[1]

Are you seeking God's favor? Are you knocking at the door of God's favor, imploring that He open it for you? If not, then why not? Our gracious Lord invites you to do exactly that.

One of the great purposes of prayer is to position yourself to receive whatever good thing God may want to give you. Those of us who have been around the block with God for a while know that, through prayer, He opens many doors of blessing that we didn't even know were there.

We may have wondered why He kept a door firmly closed that we had pleaded for Him to open. When we pray for God to show us His favor, one of the favorable things He often does is to keep tightly shut some little door we had our eye on. Instead, He opens wide some gargantuan entryway that we never even knew existed.

Because of His good favor, God opens up a vast panorama to us — a whole new level of life that we could never have imagined.

♦ ♦ ♦ WE HAVE TO ASK! ♦ ♦ ♦

For the last five years or so, I have prayed fervently that God would give my sons His favor. I want the Lord to fix His loving gaze on them, to take a keen and lively interest in them, and to freely act in kindness toward them. I want them to enjoy the greatest benefits He has to offer! So with that in mind, I have become a big-time believer in praying for the favor of God.

Now that my boys are married, my wife and I have expanded those prayers for God's favor to include Josh's wife, Kate, and Nick's wife, Meredith. Josh and Kate will soon have their first child, a boy. And yes, he will receive those prayers already for God's great gaze, favor, to be placed upon him.

In praying this way, I believe I stand in excellent biblical company, but I have to make a confession. After I began my study on the favor of God, I felt more than a little surprised to discover how many people in the Bible prayed explicitly for God's favor.

I knew they prayed for healing, for victory over enemies, for food, for children, and for uncounted numbers of other things. When I began my study on the favor of God, it escaped me how many Bible figures earnestly prayed for the favor of God.

- Jacob begged for it.[2]
- Hezekiah sought it.[3]
- Daniel petitioned for it.[4]
- Nehemiah cried out for it: *"Remember me favorably, my God,"*[5] and *"Remember me, my God, with favor."*[6]

♦ ♦ ♦ DOES GOD SHOW FAVOR TO THE WICKED? ♦ ♦ ♦

Even two kings who earned a reputation for doing evil in the eyes of the Lord started seeking God's favor after their own wickedness brought them wave after wave of trouble and anguish and despair. When God punished Jehoahaz, king of Israel, by placing him and his people under the brutal power of a hostile nation, *"Then Jehoahaz sought the LORD's favor, and the LORD heard him, for He saw the oppression the king of Aram inflicted on Israel."*[7]

A few years later, when Manasseh, the most wicked king ever to rule Judah, felt the sting of God's discipline, *"When he was in distress he sought the favor of the LORD his God and earnestly humbled himself before the God of his ancestors. He prayed to Him, so He heard his petition and granted his request."*[8] Manasseh is a good example of how God's favor comes upon both the wicked and the righteous.

Maybe you have never prayed for God's favor because you thought you did not deserve it. Do you think Jehoahaz deserved it? Do you think Manasseh deserved it? How could he, when the Bible says: *"So Manesseh caused Judah and the inhabitants of Jerusalem to stray so that they did worse evil than the nations the LORD had destroyed before the Israelites"?*[9]

Yet, when Manasseh humbled himself and repented of his sin and prayed to God and sought His favor, the Lord granted his request. He gave Manasseh His favor.

What makes you think He won't do the same thing for you?

♦ ♦ ♦ NOT ALWAYS A STRAIGHT-LINE PROPOSITION ♦ ♦ ♦

It's not only okay to seek God's favor, but it's the wise and prudent and smart thing to do. I should warn you, however, that God's favor doesn't always come to us in the manner and appearance we expect it to. Enjoying God's favor doesn't always mean a fat bank account, perfect health, an esteemed position in the community, or many other things we often assume come bundled with divine favor.

I'm guessing that no one knew this better than Joseph. You can find the complete biblical account of Joseph's life in Genesis 37–50, but I want to focus on only one aspect of his remarkable biography.

The Bible suggests that Joseph enjoyed the favor of God for most of his life. If, however, you had witnessed the hurtful events that overtook him, I doubt you would have come to that conclusion. The fact is that the favor of God does not always mean a straight line to "the good life." Very often you can enjoy the favor of God, even in the middle of extremely trying circumstances. Joseph shows us that much.

By His good favor, the Lord showed Joseph at an early age that one day he would rise to a position of great authority and power. Unwisely, Joseph blabbed about his extraordinary future to his brothers, and a short while later they reacted by stripping him of his clothes, throwing him down a dry well, and eventually selling him into slavery.

Doesn't sound much like divine favor, does it?

In time, Joseph became the slave of a wealthy Egyptian official. There in Egypt, the Bible says that *"The LORD was with Joseph, and he became a successful man."* [10] In fact, from the very moment Joseph's owner put his new slave in charge of his estate, *"The LORD blessed the Egyptian's house because of Joseph."* [11] Things were definitely looking up!

So *now* we could expect that the favor of God would sweep Joseph right up into his prophesied position of authority, couldn't we? Well, not exactly.

While Joseph never lost God's favor, he did lose the favor of his owner. When the official's wife falsely accused Joseph of attempted rape, Joseph found himself in prison. Did he still have God's favor? Yes, but he was also still a slave in a foreign land. Worse yet, now he was an exiled slave in prison. Somehow the Bible still has the audacity to say, *"While Joseph was there in the prison, the LORD was with him; he showed him kindness and granted him favor in the eyes of the prison warden."* [12]

Favored? Yes, but nevertheless in prison. In fact, Joseph remained in that dank detention center for at least two long years. [13]

God's favor does not always mean a straight line to "the good life." Sometimes, God's favor is what gets you through the difficult times. Divine favor does not always (or even usually) translate to material wealth, but it's what often gets you through your difficult moments.

In God's good time, the favor of God elevated Joseph to the second most powerful position in the mightiest nation on the face of the ancient world. All that he had dreamed as a teenager came true and in a way that neither he nor anyone in his family could ever have imaged. The capstone of the story comes in Genesis 50:20, where the mighty Joseph tells his scared-spitless brothers, *"You planned evil against me; God planned it for good to bring about the present result — the survival of many people."*

God eventually used this favored man not only to save the lives of his estranged family, but also to rescue the Egyptian people from a devastating famine. As a result, he strengthened the political position of the pharaoh — the only man who outranked him in authority.

Did Joseph enjoy the favor of God? You bet he did! He sought it as a teenager, he sought it in an Egyptian jail, and he sought it as the feared right-hand man of the pharaoh. Yet, enjoying the favor of God did not always mean comfort, wealth, or fame. Eventually he wound up with all of those things, but he didn't travel a straight line to get there. Keep that thought in mind about the favor of God as we continue our journey together. Hard times don't necessarily mean you've lost God's favor, and comfortable times don't necessarily mean you have it. If Joseph is any example for us, we learn that the favor of God can take some pretty surprising turns.

Nevertheless, it *always* leads to a spectacular destination — even if you have to wander around in the dark for a while.

◆ ◆ ◆ SEEKING OUT OF DESPERATION ◆ ◆ ◆

I did not begin to seek after God's favor until I reached a place of desperation. By the early 1990s, the Lord had blessed me with a "successful" ministry. I pastored a large and influential church . . . but I couldn't shake the feeling that *something* was missing.

It came down to a desire to passionately know God — the very same God I had pursued since my teenage years. I wanted God to tell His story through me. I didn't want to go on repeating someone else's journey. I wanted Him to create stories of my own — firsthand stories that showcased His love and power and glory, and not secondhand tales stolen from others. So that's what I prayed for.

And in response, He drove me to desperation.

I endured traumatic experiences in ministry and traumatic experiences with the health of my family.

Then God began to burden me for the nation. I sought God through fasting and prayer, and He began to imprint that burden deeply on my heart, more than ever before. Yet I still felt desperate.

Today I think of it as desperation for the genuine touch of God on my life. I wanted a true, deep, personal and soul-shaking spiritual revival. After some time spent laboring under this feeling, early one morning while I read the Scriptures, God impressed on me that I needed to journey with Him for 40 days of fasting and prayer — even though I had practiced fasting as a discipline since my college days. But that day was a whole new day. I knew God wanted to take me on a journey I'd not experienced before.

Desperation is one big reason why people seek God's favor. Maybe you feel some of that desperation right now. You want to know God in a whole new way, on a whole different dimension, and at a whole new level. If that describes you, then make the decision right now to seek the favor of God. Say it out loud: "I'm going to seek after the favor of God." I believe that God responds to a determined decision like that.

My own experience tells me that God sometimes drives us to seek His favor through suffering and trouble and the desperation that those things churn up in us. Trouble has a way of helping us to see more clearly, and to identify what we really want to be in life. If something awful happens to one of your children, you'll probably be a little more in touch with Jesus tomorrow morning than you are today! There's something about suffering and pain and illness and loss that contributes to the driving force of personal desperation.

♦ ♦ ♦ IN NEED OF FRESH, SPIRITUAL FUEL ♦ ♦ ♦

I was 30 years old when I became pastor of my current church, and I can't say that I was prepared for it. I realized quickly that I had landed in a country completely foreign to me. I couldn't pretend to be someone I wasn't. A lot of my desperation came out of emptiness. Not that I felt vacant of God! No, God was as real to me as He had ever been. Yet *I* was empty, and I knew I just *had* to feel the touch of God on my life as never before. I needed some fresh, spiritual fuel that had never filled my tank. I knew I could not do what God had called me to do without His touch — His favor. I longed for Him to fix His loving gaze upon me, to freely show me His great kindness. I needed His favor!

So I sought God. I sought His favor. I asked for His favor. I petitioned for His favor. I clamored for His favor. And you know what? He has shown me His favor. I'm convinced that He wants you to ask for the same thing.

♦ ♦ ♦ WHAT WILL BE YOUR EPITAPH? ♦ ♦ ♦

None of us lives on this earth forever. Many of us live our full three-score and ten, and some even more. Others of us check out considerably before that. But none of us sticks around for long. As James reminds us, *"You don't even know what tomorrow will bring — what your life will be! For you are a bit of smoke that appears for a little while, then vanishes."* [14]

Have you ever thought about what you want to be remembered for after you're gone? What would you like written on your epitaph? I read about a tombstone in Nova Scotia that read, "Here lies Ezekial Aikle, Age 102. The good die young." Now that was a fellow who died with his sense of humor intact!

What phrase or collection of words on your tombstone would accurately reflect the primary concern of your life? Not that I have given a lot of thought to it or have any suggestions concerning the legacy of my life, but I have thought that one of the following three epitaphs would be great on my tombstone one day (that is, if I'm worthy):

> "Making a Difference"
> "Turning the World Upside-down"
> "Remember me, my God, with favor"

I have given my life to making a difference. I want God to use me to turn the world upside-down. Yet, above all, I just want to be favored by

God. At the end, and when it is over, I hope they can write these words about me: "Remember me, my God, with favor."

A lot of what you will be remembered for depends on what you're seeking after right now. What do you spend most of your time seeking after? I know you're seeking something. It's just a matter of recognizing what and who it is. Most of us would go to great lengths to get into the presence of the president, but the chances of such a thing ever happening are slim to none. Yet every day we receive an invitation to come into the presence of the King of kings. Somehow and too often we find every reason to decline.

What epitaph will be written about your life? What are you seeking after?

One of the best epitaphs I can think of was written about a little-known man named Enoch. He lived centuries before the patriarchs Abraham, Isaac, and Jacob ever made their appearance on the earth. Enoch fathered Methuselah, the longest-lived man in the Bible. He had other sons and daughters. Other than that, we know practically nothing about him, other than one report that describes him as a prophet,[15] and the short note in Hebrews that says he pleased God.[16]

So what did Enoch seek after? The Book of Genesis leaves us in little doubt. Twice in the space of four short verses the Bible tells us simply, *"Enoch walked with God."*[17] Four little words that powerfully capture the man's legacy. *"Enoch walked with God."*

They make for a good epitaph, don't they?

I wonder, what will be your legacy? How will your children and grandchildren remember what you're seeking? What will they carve on your epitaph?

I hope my family remembers me as one who walked with God and who sought His good favor. You see, those who seek God's favor tend to leave a legacy that continues on long after they're gone. How do I know that? I know it because I've seen it. I've seen it in the lives of my contemporaries, and I've seen it in the lives of men like Joseph, who both knew God's favor and sought after it.

Long after Joseph had passed from the scene, the exciting day came when his descendants prepared to enter the Promised Land. Moses, whom God did not allow to enter at that time, pronounced an amazing blessing on the offspring of Joseph. Listen to his thrilling words:

> *May his land be blessed by the LORD*
> *with the dew of heaven's bounty*
> *and the watery depths that lie beneath;*
> *with the bountiful harvest from the sun*
> *and the abundant yield of the seasons;*
> *with the best products of the ancient mountains*
> *and the bounty of the eternal hills;*
> *with the choice gifts of the land*
> *and everything in it;*
> *and with the favor of Him*
> *who appeared in the burning bush.*
> *May these rest on the head of Joseph,*
> *on the crown of the prince of his brothers.*[18]

Wow! Yet, when Moses spoke this blessing, Joseph had been dead for centuries. Only the man's dusty old bones would make the trip with Israel into the land of Canaan.[19] Do you see what Moses was actually praying for? He was praying that the same divine favor that rested on Joseph would also rest on his many descendants.

What a good legacy! What a great epitaph! I pray this for my sons.

Why don't you, too, seek *"the favor of him who dwelt in the burning bush,"* and so bless your offspring for decades to come? Why don't you inspire the epitaph, "He sought the favor of God"? If you choose to do so, believe me, one day in heaven, you and your whole family will be glad you did.

5

DISCOVERING GOD'S FAVOR

The area where I live in northwest Arkansas is a fishing mecca. Bass, crappie, catfish, and even trout are all found in abundance in our streams, rivers, and lakes. Bass Pro Shops are all the rage, and if you don't have a boat somewhere on your property . . . well, you tag yourself as an "outsider."

A nice string of fish always reminds me that the Lord and His friends saw their own fishing careers as something more than a few fish turned over an open fire. Eternity was involved in their real "fishing careers."

Do you like to fish? After you reel something in (or you see someone else reel it in), do you like to take a step back and admire the whopper on the other end of the line? I hope so, because I'd like to encourage you to go on a fishing expedition in this chapter.

Don't worry if you don't have a boat or a good pole, because the kind of fishing expedition I want you to take does not require either. In fact, you won't need bait, a line, lures, or even water. And the kind of fish we're going after do not necessarily live in lakes and streams, do a lot of swimming, or eat worms.

No, we're going after fish a lot bigger than that. We're going after the many kinds of God's favor in your life. I want to help you identify and hold up to the bright sunlight those areas of your life where God's favor already rests on you.

By the time we are finished, I'd like you to come away with the conviction that in many ways you have tasted God's good favor in several areas of your life. That's important because sometimes we're so close to and familiar with what God already has given us of His favor that that we fail to see it as a marvelous thing. As a result, we get discouraged when difficult times surface. We tend to think, *God has forgotten all about me.*

If I can, I want to help you glimpse God's hand of favor *already* at work in your life. Maybe you've had an eye-opening experience of His favor, but you didn't recognize it. I've already told you some stories of God's hand of favor on my life, but I'm quite sure you have no interest in being me! I hope it might be encouraging to you, however, to be able to recognize the favor of God as it has enriched your life already. In fact, why don't you do this right here, in the book! Write three ways God has favored you in your life. Record them and remember them.

1.

2.

3.

That's the fish we're after in this chapter! Quite frankly, I think we all need a guide to look for such trophies because the favor of God can be difficult to recognize, even when you're right in the middle of it. It often takes more twists and turns than a bowlful of spaghetti.

My son, Josh, knows all about that.

♦ ♦ ♦ WHERE'S THE FAVOR? ♦ ♦ ♦

Several years ago, Josh graduated from Shiloh Christian School, where he enjoyed a phenomenal high school football career as the team's quarterback. Due in great measure to a new football coach and his innovative "hurry-up, no huddle" offense, Josh broke all kinds of state records in passing and total yardage, and even set two national records. In fact, one year his team had the number one offense in the nation.

Due to his success on the football field, Josh got featured many times in the statewide newspaper and once made the cover of the Arkansas football magazine. By the end of his high school career, he had received letters of interest from major universities all over the country, inquiring about the possibility of his playing for their teams.

Josh ran into one major roadblock when it came to playing major college ball, however, and that is that he stands only five feet ten inches tall — something that always raises the eyebrows of major college football coaches. They're looking for guys at least half a foot taller than that, in the belief that tall quarterbacks can more easily spot their receivers over the behemoth linemen toiling in front of them. (Don't tell Doug Flutie that; the 1984 Heisman Trophy winner from Boston College is still playing pro ball, and he is also five feet ten inches tall.)

In the end, Josh got no offers from major college teams, and wound up playing football at Ouachita Baptist University, a Division Two school. One day during a spring ballgame, when Josh was getting a real opportunity to show the coaches what he could do, he threw a phenomenal pass that his receiver caught mid-stride for a touchdown.

Right after Josh released the ball, however, a massive defensive end crushed him into the turf, giving him a major concussion. While Josh played no more in that game, everyone told him afterward, "You're going to be fine; everything's going to be cool."

Yet despite the reassurances, Josh continued to suffer major headaches. When he told his coach about them, the coach referred him to a local physician. After further tests and evaluation, the doctor recommended that Josh see a neurologist as soon as possible. After continued testing and evaluation, he then wound up at the University of Arkansas Medical Center, one of the finest hospitals in the nation for dealing with brain injuries.

As doctors studied Josh's x-rays and cat scans and MRIs, they determined that at an earlier time in his life, his brain had suffered some sort of hemorrhage. Maybe it happened as a little guy when he fell off a bike, or hit his head on the floor, or even when he suffered a football hit to the head earlier in his career. No one knew. But suddenly we had a major concern on our hands, since such an injury could easily have fatal consequences.

Yet we also had some good news. While he had suffered a major concussion, his brain had not begun hemorrhaging again. If it had begun, brain surgery would have been inevitable as well as life altering, and perhaps even life threatening.

Obviously, at that point his career as a football player was over. Despite our disappointment that he could no longer play the game he loved, we felt grateful to God that He showed us His favor in protecting our son. God used that scary incident to expose a hidden health issue that none of us knew anything about. If Josh had ever been hit in the wrong way on the field, he could have suffered a catastrophic injury. Had he been hit on the wrong side, he might never have walked again, might never have spoken again. He might even have died.

We immediately thought back to how our hearts broke for Josh when he didn't win a big-time college scholarship. At the time, we didn't see the snub as God's favor! It turned out that God was protecting our son in a way none of us had any ability to understand.

> "GOD HAS LET YOU WALK THROUGH THIS DEEP VALLEY FOR A REASON."
>
> ◆ ◆ ◆

I'll never forget telling Josh that it was all over. "Son," I said, "God has let you walk through this deep valley for a reason. But God is going to raise you up in another way at a very young age because of this. God will use this setback to set you up for Him."

Time and time again, God seems to raise up people who have suffered deep pain. Today, Josh is just two years out of college, and he holds one of the top ten high school coaching jobs in Arkansas. He's back at Shiloh Christian School, competing in the public school league with all Arkansas schools, leading his alma mater on the gridiron. After completing his first regular season as head coach at age 24, he led his very young team to the state quarterfinal game before losing and surpassing everyone's expectations. Most important, he is leading young men by his godly behavior. This dual purpose of achievement on the field and achievement in life is a partial fulfillment of his destiny, made possible by his career "detour."

All of this is the unbelievable favor of God. But you know what? At several points along the way, we had to do some serious fishing to see it!

♦ ♦ ♦ IS THE "GOOD LIFE" GOD'S FAVOR? ♦ ♦ ♦

Why does it often seem so tough to spot God's favor? One reason is that it can take on so many different attributes.

It might take the form of financial blessings, or career advancement, or community influence. Sometimes it means finding a great spouse, or drawing near to a close friend. It might mean having your basic needs met, or meeting a kind and helpful stranger. It could be as little as getting offered a cool glass of lemonade on a hot day, to as big a thing as surviving a fiery plane crash in a howling snowstorm.

Maybe you have a great business, a pretty wife or handsome husband, two kids on their way to becoming valedictorians of their classes, and a very comfortable life. Everything you touch seems to turn to gold. You're not sure what I mean when I mention a relationship with God, but you feel as if you must be on pretty good terms with "the man upstairs" in order to enjoy all the good things you have.

Is *that* the favor of God in your life? If it's not, what is it?

This may be a bigger and harder question than might first appear, for reasons that we'll investigate in just a moment. But right from the start, I hear ringing in my ears the words of James: *"Every good and perfect gift is from above, coming down from the Father of the heavenly lights."* [1] *Every* good gift is from God. *Every* perfect gift comes as a package sent from heaven.

Jesus tells us that God *"causes His sun to rise on the evil and the good, and sends rain on the righteous and the unrighteous."* [2] The sun is a good gift; so is rain. God gives them both, to the "unrighteous" as well as to the "righteous."

I recall that the apostle Paul told a group of pagans that God *"has shown kindness by giving you rain from heaven and crops in their seasons; he provides you with plenty of food and fills your hearts with joy."*[3] When people who don't even believe in the God of the Bible receive abundant rain and bumper crops and plentiful food and joy-filled hearts, all of that, too, is a good gift from God's hand.

So what is all of this about? I believe that God often uses blessings — His favor — to lure us into a closer relationship with Him. He can use *anything* to lure us into a close relationship with Him. I've met many businessmen and women who seem to have the Midas touch. Everything they do, everywhere they go, they seem to turn every opportunity into gold.

Well, who does that? God says He's the one who owns that silver and that gold.[4] So God blesses whom He wants to bless. Why does He bless the man who doesn't know Him? Just to make that man happy? No! I believe He does it to lure that man into life everlasting.

A man with wealth comes to God the same way the man with nothing comes. He comes to God through establishing a personal relationship with Jesus Christ. This happens through turning from the greatest sin of all, which is not letting Jesus be Lord, and turning in faith to Jesus Christ completely.

At this very moment, God is pursuing a relationship with every one of us. To bring us into that relationship and to help it mature, He'll do whatever it takes. If it takes extreme material blessing, He will do that. If it takes extreme tragedy, He will do that, too.

Now, don't get me wrong! God doesn't want to blast anyone with hardship. If, however, that is what it takes for some of us to wake up and realize that a close relationship with God is what life's all about, He'll do it.

Jeremiah says, *"For the Lord will not reject us forever. Even if He causes suffering, He will show compassion according to His abundant, faithful love. For He does not enjoy bringing affliction or suffering on mankind."*[5]

God won't *willingly* bring affliction or grief to us, but if that's what it takes to bring us where we need to be, He will do it unwillingly.

One Saturday evening I received a tragic phone call from the family of a young adult lady who had been killed in a car accident. I went to the family's home immediately. The young lady's mom was a godly woman. However, her dad was not a follower of Christ. Through this young woman's death, he came to Christ and was baptized, and became very active in church. The death was so tragic, yet God used the death to bring favor like never before to that family. The dad became a vibrant follower of Christ.

Is all earthly good fortune the favor of God? In some ways, I think it is. Remember what James says? *"Every perfect gift is from above."*[6] I'm sorry to say, though, that the issue seems to get a little more complicated than that. Why? Because the question immediately becomes, "Is this 'good fortune' we're talking about a good thing or a bad thing?" Think of it this way. Suppose you win $20 million in a national sweepstakes, or a long-lost, deceased uncle leaves you with at least that much in his will. Looks like a pretty good thing, doesn't it? But have you ever followed what often happens to lottery winners who go from broke to multi-millionaires overnight?

A year after a big win, many winners face a nasty divorce and property disputes. Depression and drug use ends in shattered lives. So? Was that 20 million bucks a good thing, or a bad thing? Was it from God, or from Satan?

We naturally tend to say that it was a *great* gift. Hey, if you think $20 million is a bad gift, I'll be glad to take yours!

So maybe we're asking the wrong question. Maybe we should be asking, not merely, "Where did this come from?" but much more helpful, "What has this thing produced in me?" In that way, at least we should be able to tell who's been the major influence in our life through that gift.

Here's what I mean: If this "good fortune" is creating all kinds of disharmony, rancor, and hatred in your life, then you can be sure that God had nothing to do with it. Maybe you'll never know whether that original gift came from Him or not, until you get to heaven. But what is it doing in your life *right now*? That's a question you can probably answer without too much trouble.

♦♦♦ How to Tell? ♦♦♦

So if we're trying to discover where God's hand of favor might rest on our lives, what kinds of things should we look for? How can we determine whether it's "a God thing" or a "something else thing"? How can we recognize the big fish of God's favor?

I'd like to suggest six tests to help you identify God's favor in your life. Whether you have in mind a big thing or a little thing, a material thing or a spiritual thing, a business thing or a family thing, the following six tests should give you a pretty good idea of where God's favor may be resting on you right now.

1. Do you feel a sense of internal harmony?

Regarding this "good fortune" you have, do you feel internal harmony within your family or in your soul? If your life situation appears to be full of blessing, health, and perhaps a little prosperity, does it give you a feeling of peace and harmony, or does it cause friction? Proverbs 10:22 says, *"The LORD's blessing enriches, and struggle adds nothing to it."*

So — in this area of your life, do you feel a deep sense of peace and harmony? If you do, then that's probably a pretty good indication that the Lord is intimately involved with it. His favor rests on you! If you don't — if you feel anxious and in turmoil and have to deal constantly with all kinds of disunity — then that's a pretty good indication that somebody else is involved.

2. Does this "good fortune" tend to move you toward God or away from Him?

Satan will do everything he can to keep you away from a close relationship with God, while God tenaciously pursues a closer relationship with you. Be honest. Do you feel as though the "good fortune" in your life is moving you toward God or away from Him?

Hebrews 10:22 encourages us to "draw near to God with a sincere heart in full assurance of faith" (NIV). Has your "good fortune" made this easier, or harder?

Consider the various elements of your life — great health, influential position, material blessings, financial substance, whatever — *are they keeping you from God, or pushing you toward Him?*

If a job is keeping you from that relationship, then you need to reevaluate, get your equilibrium back, and slow down long enough to get with God and recover some balance. Remember, Satan wants to take this "good thing" you have and destroy you with it. God wants to use it to bless you and those around you.

3. *Are you moving toward people or away from people?*

If you're spending more and more time with yourself, then, most likely, God has not been much involved in your "good fortune." When various blessings or pleasant circumstances lead you into withdrawal from others, the result will never be positive. Eventually, your little self-absorbed island will sink beneath the waves of a stormy, angry sea.

> SATAN WILL DO EVERYTHING HE CAN TO KEEP YOU AWAY FROM A CLOSE RELATIONSHIP WITH GOD, WHILE GOD TENACIOUSLY PURSUES A CLOSER RELATIONSHIP WITH YOU.
>
> ♦ ♦ ♦

God intends for His blessings and favor to be shared with others. The apostle Paul told some of his friends, *"You will be made rich in every way so that you can be generous on every occasion, and through us your generosity will result in thanksgiving to God."*[7] Your "good fortune" should push you into being with others, spending time with others, and blessing others. God's favor moves you into deeper relationships with others; it does not exclude them from you.

4. Do you feel content with that "good fortune," or do you feel envious?

How much is enough? When is enough, enough? Ask yourself those questions, and then take note of your answers.

If you do not feel content with what God already has given you, then your view of life has become twisted, resulting in an insatiable desire for more and more. Eventually, such a greedy habit will saddle you with an envious heart, and that kind of diseased heart will end up destroying you. Proverbs 14:30 notes, *"A tranquil heart is life to the body, but jealousy is rottenness to the bones."*

Contentedness is a clear mark of God's favor. Paul writes, *"But godliness with contentment is a great gain. For we brought nothing into the world, and we can take nothing out. But if we have food and clothing, we will be content with these."*[8] When you feel content with all that God already has given you, He is able to move you into a place of even greater favor.

5. Does your life feel ordered or disordered in this area of "good fortune"?

Take a look at your life. Do things seem to run fairly smoothly, or are you always running from one emergency to another? Does the word "organized" or "chaotic" most closely describe your life? Do you often find yourself worrying that your train is about to career off the tracks, or can you relax on the journey, despite some bumps and sharp turns along the way?

One way to tell if God or the devil has been most active in this area of "good fortune" is to take stock of the degree of order or disorder that appears to characterize your life. Satan always entices us to take the good things God gives us and twist them to selfish ends that result in disaster. Many people today seem to be living chaotic, disorderly, and unbalanced lives. That leads me to believe that they have not been enjoying God's favor as they could have. Many people do not manage well the favor of God they have been given. The Word tells us, *"God is not a God of disorder but of peace."*[9]

Whatever "good fortune" you have enjoyed has been entrusted to you for one purpose: to bring glory to God and so to bless others. This will occur, however, only when you remain balanced and orderly. For this reason, I urge you to develop a prioritized life, so that when the favor of God falls upon you, God will receive all the glory. As a result, you and those around you will reap tremendous benefits, without suffering through the chaos so characteristic of the "other side."

6. Does this "good fortune" turn your heart toward the eternal, or does it turn it toward the temporal?

Satan tries to entice us toward extremely temporal — cars, boats, a big bank account, the latest fashion, fame, a seat at the "right" table, a second home, various toys, a bigger portfolio — while God beckons us toward things eternal — heaven, glory, godly relationships, peace, joy. Where has your "good fortune" been leading you? Is it toward temporal things that will soon pass away, or toward eternal things that will remain forever?

Prolific author Rick Warren is a man who could have chosen many routes in his ministry path. As the son of a preacher, he has a great heritage. The favor of God has come upon Rick and his ministry in a very unusual manner. Why? Why Rick? Only God knows. Rick has been faithful to guide this astounding favor toward helping others by expanding God's kingdom.

God intends that all He gives you be used in some way for the expansion of His kingdom around the world. It is about God, not about you or me. It is about others, not just about you or me. It is about meeting needs and leading more and more people into a satisfying, joyful relationship with the Father of our Lord Jesus Christ.

Does that look anything like what's happened in this area of "good fortune" in your life? If so, congratulations! You've identified one major area of life where God's good favor rests on you. If not . . . then I'm afraid someone else has hijacked the train.

♦ ♦ ♦ IS GOD'S FAVOR TOUCHING YOUR LIFE? ♦ ♦ ♦

Where do you see God's favor touching your life, right now? Remember, God's favor doesn't necessarily mean a life of ease or comfort or even good health.

Have you heard the story of Joni Eareckson Tada? She broke her neck in a diving accident at 17 and has lived as a quadriplegic ever since. Yet could anyone deny that she has God's favor? The Lord has used her in countless ways over the past few decades to bless millions of people worldwide with the hope we have in Christ. God has done more with her through suffering than she could ever have accomplished with perfect health.

If you were ever to speak with Joni, you'd immediately see in her all the things we just listed as indications of God's favor — wonderful things like peace and harmony, great contentment whatever the circumstances, and a radiance that can come only from a close, personal relationship with the God of the universe. All of those things are hers in abundance.

But the question of this chapter is: *Are they yours?*

♦ ♦ ♦ FISHING FOR FAVOR ♦ ♦ ♦

It's time for you to go on your own fishing expedition. Where do you see signs of God's favor? Take some time to fish around for the divine favor that already exists in your life, a little deeper than we did previously, when you listed three areas of favor. Here I want you to reflect a little more, fish in "deeper water."

Where can you see God's favor as it already has broken out in your life? What signs do you see of His favor? What gracious things has He done for you?

How is your health? Do you have a roof over your head? Are your basic needs for food and clothing being met? Are you content with what you have? Sometimes God gives us this kind of prosperity, plus even more. Perhaps you have some of the "extras" of life. What about stocks? What about properties? What about raises or bonuses on the job?

Whatever the level of divine favor that already blesses you, God wants you to maintain a degree of order, contentedness, and balance in your life. And the only way I know to ensure this is to remember that God gave it all to you, so give it back to Him in the way He directs.

> SHARE WITH OTHERS. REMEMBER, GIVING TO GOD AND OTHERS SAVES YOU FROM SELFISHNESS AND DESTRUCTION.
>
> ♦ ♦ ♦

I hope that as you do your fishing, you will begin to recognize how good God has been to you, even in the past year. And I hope this fishing expedition sparks some gratitude on your part. I know it does within me. Many of us don't feel more grateful than we do simply because we don't go looking for the hand of God's favor on our lives.

We pine about what we don't have rather than search for what we do have. Why not turn that around, starting today? Why not look for the hand of God's favor on your life, even if your current circumstances seem less than ideal?

Nehemiah did just that, and his fishing expedition turned around a whole nation.

♦ ♦ ♦ God's Favor: A Construction Project ♦ ♦ ♦

When God has something big to do, He always puts a big vision in someone's heart. Nehemiah made this discovery firsthand.

Back in the days of ancient Israel's Babylonian captivity, God needed a wall built around His precious city Jerusalem. Yet no one in Jerusalem seemed willing to take on the job.

Hundreds of miles away, God began to put this very burden on Nehemiah's heart. Yet this man, the cupbearer to the king, could not simply go marching off to Jerusalem on a hunch. As a Jewish captive himself, he had to seek the king's permission. So he prayed, *"Give your servant success today by granting him favor in the presence"* of the king.[10]

Favor was needed.

Favor was given.

By God's favor, the king granted Nehemiah favor to go back to Jerusalem to accomplish what God had put into his heart.

After Nehemiah began his task, several powerful enemies repeatedly tried to destroy both him and his vision. The burden felt so great upon his heart that Nehemiah refused to let go of the vision. In the midst of the greatest attacks on his mission, Nehemiah sought the Lord and asked Him for favor. More than once he prayed, *"Remember me favorably, my God."*[11]

Favor requested.

Favor given.

The results? Nothing short of historic. In just 52 days, Nehemiah and his beleaguered colleagues rebuilt the entire wall around Jerusalem. How did they manage it? It happened by the favor of God, despite less than ideal circumstances.

Nehemiah overcame the small-minded people of his generation. He took a bunch of despair-filled Jews and mobilized them to greatness. As a result they did something magnificent for God. Why? Because of God's favor. When Nehemiah went fishing for favor, his nets almost burst with the huge catch he made!

Nehemiah received what each of us has the potential to receive: God's good favor. In granting us His favor, God often gives us the favor of those in authority over us, around us, and with us. God's favor enables us to do what man says is impossible. Why? *"With God,"* says the Scripture, *"All things are possible."* [12]

That is true in your life, too. Why not go on a fishing expedition to prove it to yourself? One word of caution, though: be sure to bring some heavy-duty nets!

EXPERIENCING GOD'S FAVOR

6

If you could spend an afternoon with prolific Beth Moore, I have no doubt that she would tell you she is an "ordinary" person (that's the point — aren't we all, truly?). She genuinely has a passion for helping people fulfill their spiritual longings.

More than a decade ago, Beth started Living Proof Ministries, based in Texas. Her Bible studies and conferences are literally having a worldwide impact, and she has taught across the United States and in several other countries.

Beth Moore has obvious skills that enable her to teach and communicate. It's not as if she's groping in the dark. Yet, the call on her life is bound up in this mystery we've been discussing: God favors people for certain reasons.

You don't have to be Beth Moore, and I don't have to be Billy Graham. Being willing to implement God's plan for your life is the key.

What does God's favor look like? That's a little like asking how many colors there are in the universe, or how many grains of sand dot the world's thousands of beaches.

God shows us His favor in countless ways and in limitless forms. He fixes His eye on us and shows us example after example of His gracious kindness. His favor takes so many shapes that I have trouble accurately defining and describing it.

*I*n this chapter, I'd like to take you on a short tour of the kinds of divine favor I've seen expressed in the lives of a few people close to me. Every person you'll meet has a life different from all the others, yet every one of them has seen God bless him or her with His favor — and from a short distance away, I've seen it and marveled at it and rejoiced in it. How exciting! Let's glimpse some of the same things I have witnessed, just to give you a hint of the kind of favor that might be waiting right around the bend, for *you*.

♦ ♦ ♦ THE MANY FLAVORS OF FAVOR ♦ ♦ ♦

Financial Favor

When I think of the favor of God, I can't help but think of my friend J.B. Hunt. Perhaps you've seen the countless trucks around the country that bear his name.

Many years ago, J.B. received the Lord, married a Christian queen named Johnelle, and both remain very active in our church. If you wanted to find the personification of the American dream and a good picture of what free enterprise can accomplish, you could hardly do better than look at the lives of J.B. and Johnelle. In his younger years, J.B. was a truck driver and a dreamer. His dreams drove him to build something out of the ordinary.

One day he got out from behind the wheel and began a trucking company. Through the years his business grew, and eventually he took the company public. Today, the company operates in the billions of dollars. This down-to-earth man with an elementary school education could teach the most educated people in the world a thing or two about vision and dreaming. He was willing to take a risk — and he still is, even as his birthdays climb past the mid-70 mark. Today, he no longer directs and manages J.B. Hunt Transport. Since leaving there several years ago, he has been involved in almost 50 businesses, many of which he started himself. He never, ever quits!

It seems to me that J.B. has a unique ability to make money. Why? I think it's because he enjoys the favor of God. He reads through the Bible every 18 months or so. He never misses church unless he's out of town. Back in the days when he and Johnelle hardly had a dime to their name, they still gave God at least one-tenth of their income, and today they continue that practice.

J.B. and Johnelle Hunt are two blessed people. God has enriched them, not merely with the material things of this world, but with something far greater: His favor. It just seems to me as if God's loving gaze remains fixed upon their lives.

The favor of God does not always translate into visible "success," however, such as a fat bank account, big promotion, or similar gaudy things. Mostly, it translates into God's active, concerned presence in a life. It involves His gracious provision.

Favor in Crisis

When I think of the favor of God and how He showers it down upon various people in various ways, I think about my friend Cheryl Lyall. Over the years, Cheryl and Jeana have established a relationship. She has always been loving and extremely supportive to our family as well as to our church. Some years ago, after much prayer, her husband came to know Jesus Christ as Lord and Savior. He had an immediate and dramatic change in lifestyle. He not only started coming to church, but he soon became involved in various levels of leadership.

One evening I received a tragic phone call, the kind you never want to get. Cheryl's husband had been killed instantly in an automobile accident.

I will never forget visiting her home that evening. The entire front yard was filled with loving friends whose lives had been deeply affected by this entire family. I really believe that much of that incredible support that evening and in the ensuing days came because of the influence of Cheryl Lyall on countless people.

Cheryl is now a single woman, and widow, who had depended upon her husband for all those years. The very thing that she had prayed for, the transformation of her husband, had occurred. But now he was gone.

The great news is that God saw the big picture. He was one day going to call her husband home. When that day came, he was prepared to enter eternity.

The amazing thing about Cheryl Lyall today is that her needs are met. She is so in love with the Word of God and with the people of God. She loves to mark her Bible with that phrase, "the favor of God." She understands and experiences God's favor. You see, God's favor doesn't always come in the form of extreme wealth or international influence; but it does come in the most important areas of life: provision for your needs, even in times of sorrow and grief. She is a great illustration of someone who has experienced the favor of God.

Dr. Harold O'Chester has a remarkable story. During the time Harold attended seminary and pastored a church part-time on the weekends, he and his entire family suffered a serious car accident. Only he survived. That obviously provoked a lot of questions in his hurting heart! At the same time, he stayed faithful to God, despite his disastrous ordeal. And God's favor helped him through that tragedy and the deep sorrow he felt for years.

> OVER AND OVER, WE SEE GOD'S FAVOR DEMONSTRATING ITSELF THROUGH THE GREATEST NEEDS OF LIFE.
>
> ◆ ◆ ◆

Building Strong Marriages

Harold continued to attend seminary, and eventually the Lord brought a woman into his life. Barbara had never been married, the two of them fell in love, and soon they became husband and wife. Eventually they brought three children into the world, all of them now grown up and married.

Through their church in Austin, Texas, they developed a marriage retreat ministry. It started just for the people of their church, but soon grew to expand across the South. The Lord blessed their desire to build marriages and families, and eventually they branched out. She began to do retreats for women, while he led retreats for men. Barbara gained unusually strong influence among women in the South, among whom she ministered to thousands annually.

Their lives have always demonstrated a great commitment, first to the Lord, and then to the embattled institutions of marriage and family. Without question, it was through the favor of God that Harold found Barbara. *"A man who finds a wife finds a good thing,"* declares Proverbs 18:22, *"and obtains favor from the LORD."*

The favor of God rested upon them as a couple and opened up many doors to needy places where they could identify with suffering and pain and challenges, and yet offer the hope and healing of God.

Bert Miller and his wife, Wanda, were members of our church when we served at the First Baptist Church of Palacios, Texas. Bert owned some Texaco distributorships in that coastal city. After I came to Springdale as pastor, we started building a large worship center. I decided we needed someone with the skills to take over administration of the entire massive complex, both the facilities and the grounds. God put Bert on my heart.

Out of the blue, Bert sold those distributorships and he and his wife moved to Springdale. They've been with us since 1988. It has delighted my heart to see the incredible favor God has given him with our people. Because he's such an average guy, he fits in very well with everyone. Over the years he has so consistently proven his faithfulness to the Lord that God just seems to constantly increase his responsibilities. Over the past 18 years, and especially over the last 10, Bert has become one of my closest confidants. Now he has the privilege of helping to design and to oversee, in the next two years, the building of facilities that will enable our church family to reach greater numbers of people for God.

Here's a guy who owned some Texaco distributorships in a small coastal city in Texas (population 4,000), but who wakes up today and makes a huge difference for the kingdom of God. And these days his son goes literally all over the world, sharing the gospel, making a difference, expanding the kingdom of God, helping people both with humanitarian and gospel efforts. I see Bert as a tremendous example of the favor of God.

Then there's coach Gus Malzhan, who grew up in Fort Smith, Arkansas. Gus bounced from college to college, trying to play football, and finally graduated from Henderson State University. He ended up becoming the defensive coordinator at a small public school in northeast Arkansas.

After one year, the head coach left, and Gus always says the only reason he got hired as the new head coach was because no one else applied. (When you consider where the school is located, you have to say there could be some truth to that.)

Within a couple of years he started winning, and winning *big*. He went to the state championship football game and lost. Then our school lost its head football coach, and we asked Gus to join us.

Gus came in at the right place, at the right time, as the right man with the right players, and quickly formulated a hurry-up, no-huddle, fast-paced offense, which quickly transformed all of Arkansas high school football. His teams broke national records; and in the process, Gus gained all kinds of national attention. Gus led us in a 44-game winning streak and won two state championships at Shiloh. One night, little Shiloh Christian School played the largest high school in all of Arkansas, in front of thousands of fans — and ended up tying them, 7-7.

Not too long afterward, the coach at that school retired, and we lost Gus to the bigger program. In his first year at Springdale High School, he had to play Shiloh Christian in Razorback Stadium. That night, more than 24,000 people saw the game, the largest crowd ever to attend an Arkansas high school football contest; Springdale High defeated Shiloh, 21-14.

In his second year at Springdale High, he led his team to the state championship game, but lost. At the time I write, he's completed his fourth season, with his team ranked nationally.

This is what the favor of God can look like. Here's this normal guy from Fort Smith, Arkansas, who happened to be at the right place at the right time. He positioned himself for success, and today Gus could literally go anywhere he wanted to go. Some college opportunities have already come his way, but he's not chosen to move up to the college ranks; I suspect that one day he will.

I tell him constantly, "Gus, you just have God's favor on your life and career." I am one of his biggest fans, and I count both him and his wife, Kristy, dear friends, along with their sweetheart girls, Kylie and Kensie. His entire family remains active in our church. He is a great illustration from the world of sports of a guy who has God's favor on his life. Whatever he does, that divine favor just seems to stick close by.

Does any of this kind of divine favor look good to you? If it does, then in the last section of this book I'd like to suggest what you can do to set yourself up to experience your own flavor of God's favor. If you want to know what it might taste like for you, keep reading.

♦ ♦ ♦ WHO CAN COUNT THEM? ♦ ♦ ♦

I don't know what God's favor is going to look like in your life, any more than any observer could have predicted what it would look like in Esther's life. I don't know what flavor of God's favor will ultimately bless you and yours. Baskin-Robins has thirty-two flavors of ice cream. How many flavors exist of the favor of God? Who knows?

The best we can do, I think, is to echo 1 Peter 4:10, which reminds us of "God's grace in its various forms" (NIV). I have no idea what shape God's favor might take in your life, or what flavor it could be. But I *do* know He urges you and beckons you and encourages you to find it, taste it, and experience it in all its fullness.

How can you best position yourself to receive it? Let's talk about that next.

PART THREE

POSITIONING
FOR GOD'S
FAVOR

Our Heavenly Father bestows His gracious favor on those He chooses for purposes of His own. While His purposes often look very mysterious to us, it remains true that we can so position ourselves to make it much more likely that He will bless us with His favor. Throughout history, godly men and women have done just that. This section is designed to take you to a whole different level of pursuing the favor of God.

7

THROUGH GROWING

Mel Gibson might have been snubbed by the Academy of Motion Pictures for 2005, but he no doubt is happy to trade an Oscar for the global impact his landmark film, The Passion of the Christ, has had.

When he announced that he would produce and direct the film, Gibson did it, in spite of being mocked and reviled by much of the entertainment community. He spent his own money to create this remarkable story. He pounded the pavement, promoting the film everywhere he could.

The interesting thing about the interviews Gibson sat for revolves around this idea that he felt compelled to do it. He knew it would cost him in certain ways. Some Hollywood producers went on record that they would never work with the controversial star again. He did it anyway.

Ultimately, it doesn't matter what his motives were (although he made quite a good case for all that); the film resulted in changed lives around the world. He gave audiences the opportunity to see and hear biblical languages spoken exclusively. The moving and brutal death of Jesus Christ was obviously a work of the Holy Spirit.

One could argue that Gibson already had it all, and in fact didn't risk anything. He's rich, handsome, famous, a power player in a tough town. I would argue that he risked a lot. Ridicule can be a crushing burden for any of us. Ridicule on an international stage is something beyond that.

*G*ibson had somewhat the same experience as Job. His reputation suffered, his family was attacked, and he was stressed. But at the end of the ordeal, God gave to him much more materially than he had before. *The Passion of the Christ* grossed almost $400 million domestically, more than ten times what it cost to make. Financial gain should never be our real agenda, but it's interesting that God at times chooses to bless in this way. Gibson could not have had this as his motivation because of the widespread uncertainty about how the film would be perceived. He could have lost his proverbial shirt.

I'm intrigued that Gibson was like the prophet Isaiah. Both were willing to spread God's word to a cynical audience. His many years of experience and training in filmmaking prepared him, and when the time came for *The Passion of the Christ,* the actor stood up and was counted. He had grown through the years for just such a moment.

Are you growing toward your destiny? The man must be quite a guy who can serve as the model for a memorable part of the biography of Jesus Christ.

You probably recognize the following words as a literary sketch of Jesus' boyhood years: *"And Jesus increased in wisdom and stature, and in favor with God and with people."* [1] What you may not recognize is that the sentence is almost word-for-word an echo on the life of a young Israelite who lived many centuries earlier.

Listen to the Bible's description of this famous predecessor to Jesus: *"The boy Samuel grew in stature and in favor with the LORD and with men."* [2]

What made Samuel a fitting candidate to prefigure the life of Christ? How did he grow in favor with God? Let's investigate those two crucial questions as we look briefly into the early life of the man who became known as Samuel the prophet.

♦ ♦ ♦ LESSONS FROM THE LIFE OF SAMUEL ♦ ♦ ♦

At the top, we should remind ourselves of the greatness of this man. How favored was Samuel? Many centuries after he had passed from the scene, and just before the Lord destroyed Judah for its sin and rebellion, God told the prophet Jeremiah, *"Even if Moses and Samuel should stand before Me, My compassions would not reach out to these people."* [3]

That's pretty heady company!

Wouldn't you like to be mentioned in the same breath with Moses, the man who spoke with God *"face to face, just as a man speaks with his friend"*? [4] I would! So what made Samuel such a favorite of God? How did he "grow in favor" with the Lord, even as a boy? Perhaps we can learn from him what sorts of things it takes to secure the best chance of attracting the favor of God.

1. He had a good start in life.

Samuel's very existence can be traced to his mother's desperate prayer. So at a very young age, his parents dedicated him to God. His mother, Hannah, told Eli the priest, *"I prayed for this boy, and since the LORD gave me what I asked Him for, I now give the boy to the LORD. For as long as he lives, he is given to the LORD."* [5]

In Samuel's case, that meant the boy grew up literally in the shadow of the ark of the covenant, living in the tabernacle of God then located in Shiloh. From his earliest memories, Samuel lived and breathed the things of God.

You might not have enjoyed such a spiritually rich upbringing, but you can take steps right now to create a home filled with the sweet aroma of God. You might not have enjoyed such a godly home as a child, but you can create one starting today for your own children and grandchildren. If you would like to attract the favor of God, I can think of few things that would give you a better chance of success.

2. Samuel treated the things of God with great respect.

While Eli effectively trained young Samuel in the ways of God, the old priest enjoyed far less success with his own sons. The Bible says that Eli's adult children badly abused their fellow Israelites and treated the Lord's offering "with contempt." In direct opposition to this report, it says of Samuel, *"The boy Samuel served in the LORD's presence."* [6]

How many of us treat the Lord's things with contempt? When we complain, gossip, criticize the Lord's servants, and manipulate the Lord's people, how can we wonder if we see so little of the Lord's favor?

3. Samuel grew up in the presence of God.

As Samuel grew taller and heavier and heard his voice grow deeper, he saw his arms grow stronger. He made the Lord his constant companion. He did not live merely in the presence of a few sacred artifacts, but he lived in the very presence of the Living God. The Bible tells us quite simply, *"The boy Samuel grew up in the presence of the LORD."*[7]

Something happens to you when you "grow up" in the presence of the Lord, whether you're 7 years old or 70. You increasingly understand the true nature of life. You recognize how small you are and how infinite is God. You begin to grasp that nothing in the universe is more important than God's glory, and that He invites you to display it to the world, and one day share in it yourself.

Someone who "grows up" in the presence of the Lord, who regularly breathes in the brisk air of heaven, who walks with God and talks with God and introduces others to God, very likely will experience a great deal of the favor of God. Samuel did! There's no reason you can't do the same.

4. Samuel made it a practice to listen to God and obey what He said.

Because of the wickedness of Eli's sons, God promised to *"raise up a faithful priest for Myself. He will do whatever is in My heart and mind."*[8] Who was that "faithful priest"? Samuel!

Even as a young boy, Samuel learned to listen for the Lord's voice and then to act on what he heard. Toward the beginning of his life, he didn't always recognize or understand God's call.[9] But he kept at it. He listened to his instructors, and practiced what he learned. Before long, he had become a faithful priest who habitually did what was on the heart and mind of God Almighty.

Do you want to position yourself to receive the favor of God? Then do what Samuel did. It was Jesus himself, remember, who told us, *"If anyone loves Me, he will keep My word. My Father will love him, and We will come to him and make Our home with him."* [10] That, my friend, is a huge, flashing billboard to divine favor!

5. Samuel kept growing in his faith.

I can't overstate the importance of the text that began our discussion: *"The boy Samuel grew in stature and in favor with the LORD and with men."* [11] Samuel *grew* in his relationship with God. He continued to take steps forward, to learn new lessons, to take risks, to mature in his faith. He didn't allow himself to stagnate or to say, "I think I've come far enough in my spiritual life. I believe it's time for a long vacation."

6. Are you growing in your faith?

Do you rely more on the Lord today than you did five years ago? Are you pushing yourself in any areas of spiritual discipline that don't necessarily come easily to you? Do you meet daily with the Lord to see what new adventure He might have for you? Are you faithfully following the guidance of God's Word when it tells you to *"grow in the grace and knowledge of our Lord and Savior Jesus Christ"*? [12]

If you want to position yourself to receive and enjoy the favor of God, you will if you're not already doing so. If the example of Samuel is any guide at all for you and me, we won't delay another day.

♦ ♦ ♦ A HUMBLE HEART ♦ ♦ ♦

The story of Samuel shows us that while God places His favor on men and women by His sovereign choice, yet we can position ourselves by developing the right attitudes and actions. How? By becoming far more likely candidates to receive and enjoy the favor of God. In other words, while God makes His choices, He often allows us to influence those choices.

So the question is: What kinds of attitudes and actions tend to attract the favorable attention of God? What can we do, and what kind of people can we be as we seek to give ourselves the best chance of receiving His gracious favor? What tends to attract the favor of God?

I admit that I have a tendency to start with the things we can "do," before focusing on the things we can "be." But no doubt that's getting the cart before the horse, and the caboose before the engine.

Before we start talking about appropriate actions, we should consider our attitudes. It was Jesus, I recall, who said, *"For from the heart come evil thoughts, murders, adulteries, sexual immoralities, thefts, false testimonies, blasphemies."* [13]

Nothing we "do" will make much of a difference if we don't first get our hearts on the right path, for our attitudes determine the worth of our actions. What attitude seems most likely to attract the favorable attention of God? I doubt there is any attitude with more power to turn His head in our direction than "humility."

♦ ♦ ♦ THE PROBLEM WAS ME! ♦ ♦ ♦

I learned how much God loved a humble heart in 1995. Through some deep moments of seeking the Lord during a tough 40-day window, God revealed to me the deep-seated, ugly pride in my heart.

On one very long Saturday, God would not let me sleep for almost the entire night. He used that uncomfortable time to show me that the greatest problem in my walk with God was *me*. The greatest problem in my church was *me*. The greatest problem in my ministry was *me*. Through confessing and repenting of my pride, both privately and publicly, God began the journey of building in me a more humble heart.

What does it mean to be humble? One definition I like says that humility prompts us to lay low before God. *"I live in a high and holy place, and with the oppressed and lowly of spirit, to revive the spirit of the lowly and revive the heart of the oppressed."* [14]

God often contrasts His lofty position with our lowly one, but promises to lift us up if we will humbly bow down. So no wonder Paul counsels us, *"No one should deceive himself. If anyone among you thinks he is wise in this age, he must become foolish so that he can become wise. For the wisdom of this world is foolishness with God, since it is written: He catches the wise in their craftiness — and again, The Lord knows the reasonings of the wise, that they are futile. So no one should boast in men."* 15

The Bible hammers us on this issue of humility and pride. *"God resists the proud, but gives grace to the humble,"* says James 4:6. And then, almost as if to see if we heard him, just four verses later he adds, *"Humble yourselves before the Lord, and He will exalt you."* 16 When God "lifts you up," James declares, He's showing you His favor.

So do you want His favor? If you do, then you will reject foolish pride and humble yourself before God. A humble heart admits that this thing is really not about me, but about God. Several popular Christian authors, such as Rick Warren and Max Lucado, recently have reminded us that, "It's not about me." Such a statement flies in the face of a "me-culture," a "me-church," and a "me-generation." In my opinion, self-absorption represents one of the greatest threats to our nation's spiritual security. It really is *not* about me. It is *not* about you. It is *not* about us.

It is about *God*. A humble heart understands that it is about God . . . and about no one and nothing else.

Peter wanted to make sure that we heard this message, so in his first book he writes, *"Humble yourselves therefore under the mighty hand of God, so that He may exalt you in due time."* 17 Peter's admonition sounds a lot like the one in James, but Peter's may stir my soul even more, because of the two additional thoughts he spotlights.

While James tells us to humble ourselves "before the Lord," Peter counsels us to humble ourselves "under God's mighty hand." So what's the difference? Touch! Peter pictures the Lord's hand upon him, touching him. He almost seems to be asking us, "Do you want God's hand of favor on you? Or will you insist on His hand of discipline?" How I want the mighty touch of God on my life, especially when it overflows with His favor! Don't you?

Second, while James promises simply that God "will lift you up," Peter declares that the Lord "may" do so "in due time." Peter does not want his readers to misunderstand and think that if they do A, God is immediately obligated to do B.

WE CAN MUCH BETTER POSITION OURSELVES TO RECEIVE GOD'S FAVOR BY HUMBLING OURSELVES BEFORE HIM.

God is sovereign, and He parcels out His favor whenever and to whomever He chooses. Still, Peter insists, we can much better position ourselves to receive God's favor by humbling ourselves before Him. When God sees a humble heart, He smiles. And when He smiles, there's no telling what He may do next!

Have you ever noticed that in both of these texts, the burden is laid upon *us* to humble *ourselves*? It is not God humbling us, even though He can, and He has, and He will if we won't. It is about us taking the initiative to humble ourselves before God. How do we do this?

1. **We sit**. A humble heart sits at the feet of Jesus, listening carefully to His counsel, as Mary did when the Master visited her house.[18]

2. **We wait**. A humble heart waits for God to reveal His plan of attack, rather than scurrying around to set its own agenda. Such waiting does not mean doing nothing; rather, it means doing all you can *in faith*, but refusing to rush ahead into any area without the sense that God is leading you there.[19]

3. **We act.** A humble heart takes action according to God's direction, not necessarily its own. Although God calls us both His children and His friends, He alone reigns as the Lord of the universe. So Jesus tells us, *"Go, therefore, and make disciples of all nations, baptizing them in the name of the Father and of the Son and of the Holy Spirit, teaching them to observe everything I have commanded you. And remember, I am with you always, to the end of the age."*[20]

Humility loves to obey, and it does not fear to be considered weak for doing so. In fact, it understands that God seems to be attracted to weakness, as author Jim Cymbala noted in his book *Fresh Wind, Fresh Fire*. Why? As a surprised apostle Paul discovered, God's power is made perfect in weakness.[21]

So do you want to enjoy God's favor? Then make yourself a prime candidate for it by humbling yourself, even if that makes you seem weak in the eyes of others. Don't let the opinion of men keep you from experiencing the favor of God! Instead, humble yourself and remember Paul's wise conclusion on the topic: *"Therefore, I will most gladly boast all the more about my weaknesses, so that Christ's power may reside in me."* [22]

♦ ♦ ♦ A HUNGRY HEART ♦ ♦ ♦

God also takes great delight in what I call a "hungry" heart. He promises to give His full attention to the spiritually hungry, to those who seek Him with their whole hearts. [23]

"Blessed are those who hunger and thirst for righteousness, because they will be filled," Jesus promised. [24] "As a deer longs for streams of water, so I long for You, God," declared the Psalmist. [25]

I believe a hungry heart reveals itself in at least three regular habits, or spiritual disciplines:

♦ ♦ ♦ A DAILY TIME WITH GOD ♦ ♦ ♦

God is very attracted to the person who eagerly puts himself before the Lord, day after day. The Psalmist repeatedly says things like, *"At daybreak, LORD, You hear my voice."* [26] Jesus himself often sought the Father in prayer before dawn. [27] So if He, the Son of God who has unlimited power, chose to practice this discipline, who are we to think we don't need it?

Remember J.B. Hunt, whom you met in the last chapter? A long time ago, he made it a practice to read the Bible from cover to cover. These days as he reads the Word, he often writes a note or prayer to his children or grandchildren, entrusting it to one of them as a direct letter from God and from him. The man is 78 years old!

As a junior or senior in high school, I made the commitment to have a regular time with God. Humbly I say to you, I cannot remember the last time when I did not start my day in God's Word and talking to the Lord. I really believe this has been a spiritual secret in my life.

I have seen it grow and deepen through the years and become more meaningful.

What at one time might simply have been a practice of discipline, today is a non-negotiable conviction. Before CNN, before *USA Today*, before anything else, I begin every day with God. In fact, I learned years ago (and spoke about it in my book on prayer), that you put Jesus first, or you get nothing in life. Yes, it's Jesus first.

Back in the '80s, I began to push myself to reach a brand new level with God in my devotional life. Since then, five days a week, I've gotten up at 4 a.m. to spend at least the first hour with God, listening to what His Word says to me. I did not work on manuscripts or books or messages to others. Let me set the record straight: I am *not* a morning person! You should know that I like to stay up late, and I prefer to sleep in to some degree. But I've trained myself to get up early because I want to spend that time with God.

After this, until about 10:30 a.m., I remain in my study. After that, I exercise and then make some kind of luncheon meeting. This discipline of putting God and His Word first in my life has changed my life. Yes, the vast majority of that time from Sunday through Thursday is used for the purpose of preparing to speak at various venues and for other ministry responsibilities, but the secret is to begin your day with God. On Fridays and Saturdays, I usually sleep until seven or eight a.m., but I always begin my day with God.

If you have not already done so, make a commitment today to make a daily appointment with God. Read His Word regularly, talk to Him, and even write letters to Him. These daily practices will help position you to receive God's unusual favor.

♦ ♦ ♦ A STRONG DESIRE TO LIVE OUT GOD'S WILL ♦ ♦ ♦

By a choice of the will and through the power of the Spirit, a person with a hungry heart longs to echo the words of Jesus: *"My food is to do the will of him who sent Me,"* [28] and *"I do not seek My own will, but the will of Him who sent Me."* [29] He feels hungry to live life God's way.

I have met many men who felt led by God to leave a certain region of the country, yet because Mom and Dad lived 30 miles away, they refused to leave. I believe that our willingness to do what God wants us to do — to obey Him and follow the clear promptings of His Spirit — is another factor in His choice to place His hand of favor on our lives.

> A PERSON WITH A HUNGRY HEART WANTS, MORE THAN ANYTHING, TO LIVE OUT GOD'S WILL.
>
> ♦ ♦ ♦

You can't very well do the will of God if you don't know it. You must get yourself intimately familiar with what His Word says. Neither can you do the will of God by relying on your own strength. You need to learn how to tap into the power of the Holy Spirit. When you learn to practice these habits, you'll be ready to join the "Just Say Yes Club of God" — so that whatever He asks, you'll answer with a quick, "Yes!"

♦ ♦ ♦ AN EAGERNESS TO BE WITH GOD'S PEOPLE ♦ ♦ ♦

A person with a hungry heart delights to move among God's people. She craves the fellowship and worship and instruction and encouragement she finds there. She longs to see what God is doing among her friends. Healthy church relationships mean a healthy life, and a healthy heart means a vibrant life full of healthy church relationships.

Hebrews 10:25 advises us: *"Let us not give up meeting together, as some are in the habit of doing, but let us encourage one another — and all the more as you see the Day approaching"* (NIV).

Jesus wants His church to become the people and the place where you find the greatest encouragement to your spiritual life. Jesus loves His church and died for His church. The Bible even calls the church the bride of Jesus Christ, thus declaring His unconditional love for it.[30]

How can we not love His church?

How can we not worship in His church?

How can we not serve through His church?

How can we not minister to a hurting world through His church?

How can we not get involved in a Bible-believing, evangelistic, ministry-driven church?

When you give the church its rightful place in your life, you position yourself for God's favor. Please, take this counsel: you will never become all God wants you to be, or receive all of the favor He wants to give you, until you begin to love the church that Jesus died to create.

♦ ♦ ♦ LET'S GET IN POSITION ♦ ♦ ♦

Scripture is full of people who positioned themselves to receive the favor of God. They form a happy part of that great cloud of witnesses who urge us on to do the same.

The plain fact is that men and women who adjust their attitudes and behaviors to get in alignment with the teaching of Scripture, position themselves to enjoy the favor of God more than those who do not. How many people have you known who complain that, spiritually, they are just stopped in the water, not moving. Then you find out through a series of questions that there is no prayer life and no Bible reading. Those who achieve in life are those who have that fire in the belly.

That doesn't mean that if you behave in a certain way and cultivate a certain kind of attitude, that God is obligated to lavish His favor on you in the way you think best. Still, those who cultivate a humble, hungry heart are far more likely to experience the wonders of God's favor than those who just don't care.

Don't think I'm just blurting out words here! I'm trying to practice what I preach. I want to cultivate a humble heart, a hungry heart, and a healthy heart. As I do, I wait with great expectation to discover what God is going to do next in my life. So I have learned to rest in Him and in whatever He may choose to do with me.

I don't mind telling you that five years ago, I wasn't "here." I did not have the right perspective. Today, however, if God wants to lead me in some unforeseen way that doesn't appear to fit in with my current plans, so be it. I've seen so much of His unexpected favor in the past five years that I know better than to try to prescribe what He "needs" to do or "ought" to do. He's God!

You know what? I've learned that's a very, VERY good thing.

THROUGH FAITHFULNESS

When Esther Su immigrated to the United States from her native Hong Kong, she took advantage of the great opportunities in this country. She finished a Ph.D. in biochemistry from the University of Michigan and looked forward to a wonderful career. She purposed in her heart to use the talents she had to better the world.

While in college she began to think about spiritual things. Her intellect was stretching and growing, and soon her spiritual life was also. Meeting fellow immigrant William Ho, Esther decided there might be an alternate plan for her life. They married and eventually Dr. William Ho and Dr. Esther Su (Chinese women almost always keep their maiden names) became the proud parents of four bright, beautiful children who — you guessed it — obtained doctorate after doctorate.

Today, Esther sees the beauty that has emerged from her faithfulness to the God she found in college ("I gave myself to God the Creator"). Along with William, she led the children along the right paths, and the couple delight in the accomplishments of Samuel, Adina, Susanna, and Sean. The home their mother made provided a wonderful environment for spiritual growth for the entire family.

♦ ♦ ♦ Are You Being Faithful to God's Plan for Your Life? ♦ ♦ ♦

L ast year I saw an amazing thing happen in our church. We were entering into a multi-million dollar fundraising program in order to finance Phase One of our growing ministry at Pinnacle Hills. We also wanted to provide additional facilities at our Springdale campus. The financial need dwarfed anything I have ever taken on.

I felt compelled to take the lead in this project, which we called Special Treasures. We decided not to hire an outside fundraising company to assist us, and instead I tried to get in front of every active adult member of the church. For two solid months, Jeana and I hopped in our car to speak at special gatherings that typically featured less than a hundred people apiece. Most of the time these meetings took place in someone's home several nights each week.

I wanted to start out with the senior adults who attend our Springdale campus, and I spoke to a few hundred of them at a lunch meeting. As I laid out the need to this faithful group that had paid such a heavy price to make this church what it is, I felt invigorated by their enthusiasm and support.

At the end of the meeting, Jeana introduced me to a lady I'll call "Mrs. G." This somewhat feeble woman had a hard time speaking clearly. She had shown Jeana a ring, which she placed in my hand. "Pastor," she told me in a faltering voice, "this is all I can give. It's the best I have."

Then she told me that she would not be able to be present at the end of the project, since she was about to move to an adjoining state. Before she left, however, she wanted to present me with her gift. Never before or since had I experienced such a feeling. Her faithfulness just took away my breath.

Over the next several days, as I met with other groups, I kept thinking about my memorable encounter with this faithful senior. By my third meeting, I decided to take the ring and tell of my encounter with Mrs. G I described how this elderly lady had given all she had to give, and then

I said, "If she could do this, why can't we give something great? Surely someone here tonight would be willing to give $5,000 for this ring." I went home that night without getting a response.

The next morning, one of our men e-mailed me to tell me that God had kept him up most of the night, putting it on his heart to give $5,000 for that ring. Once more I felt absolutely astounded.

That night I took the ring to the next meeting and told the story of Mrs. G, her ring, and the $5,000 pledge. I said, "Surely someone here tonight wants to give $10,000 for this ring; and when you get the ring, will you please give it back to Special Treasures? Because God may not be finished with it yet."

After the meeting as I was walking out, a couple came up to me and said, "As soon as you said that, we knew that was us. Tomorrow morning, by the time you get to work, Pastor, there will be a $10,000 check to Special Treasures for the ring."

I began to tell the story again and again. Over the next many nights, that ring helped us raise $20,000, and then $40,000, and then $80,000, and then $160,000. The day before the commitment ceremony, that ring sold for $1,043,000. The whole experience just blew me away. In the end, the ring brought in a total of $1,358,000 to our Special Treasures effort.

When Mrs. G placed that ring in my hand, little did we know how enormously her faithful action would attract the favor of God. Her faithfulness turned into fruitfulness. That story became the rallying cry for our entire Special Treasures fundraising effort and helped encourage our people to give more than $25 million, above what they give regularly to the ministry of our church — at least four times greater than any amount ever committed at our church toward a building program.

The faithfulness of Mrs. G fueled the success of our Special Treasures program. Her faithfulness not only demonstrated the favor of God, it also attracted it beyond measure — both to our church and to her, personally. Once she relocated to another city, our church helped her financially. The sad news is that, just recently, Mrs. G died. She had told me she would never return, and she didn't. But she is now in heaven with the Lord, receiving her rewards. The Lord will reward her great faithfulness to be willing to give all she had, even though what she had was limited. God will remember her faithfulness. Faithfulness positions us to receive the favor of God.

♦ ♦ ♦ A GREAT WAY TO GET NOTICED ♦ ♦ ♦

We've already seen that developing a humble, hungry heart can powerfully attract the favorable attention of God. While that's a wonderful strategy to pursue, it's not the only one. In this chapter, I'd like to suggest an additional route to the same fantastic destination.

We could call it the *Freeway of Faithfulness*. Those wise enough to travel along this route are almost sure to attract the favorable attention of God. Just as people from many walks of life took note of the faithfulness of Mrs. G, so God notices and appreciates all those who determine to live as faithful followers of the King of kings.

Do you want to position yourself to receive the favor of God? If so, I'd like to suggest that personal faithfulness become another big item on your "to do" list. I think that a woman named Mary is just the person to show you what I mean.

♦ ♦ ♦ THE EXAMPLE OF MARY ♦ ♦ ♦

If you wanted to identify the one woman in history who received more of God's favor than anyone else, your search would quickly narrow to a young woman named Mary. Without question, she gets the all-time blue ribbon for the favor of God.

Who else, after all, did God choose to become the mother of Jesus Christ? Who else did God pick to bear the Savior of the world?

Other than the few things recorded about her in the New Testament, we know next to nothing about Mary. Most scholars think she was probably about 16 years of age when she learned that God would bring the Messiah into the world through her, but no one knows for sure. What we do know about her centers around the word "favored."

The first time she appears in the Bible, the angel Gabriel greets her with a hearty, *"Greetings, you who are highly favored! The Lord is with you."* [1] So we learn that not only does she enjoy God's favor; in fact, she is *highly* favored. Moments later, Gabriel re-emphasizes her lofty status in heaven by telling her, *"You have found favor with God."* [2]

No sooner does Gabriel disappear than Mary hurries off to see her elderly cousin, Elizabeth — by then, six months pregnant with another miracle baby — the one we know as John the Baptist. Once again, Mary hears about her favored status. Her expectant cousin greets her with the delightful question, "Why am I so favored, that the mother of my Lord should come to me?"[3]

Hands down, we can rightfully call Mary the "favored one."

But how did she get the privilege? What caused her to receive such favor from the Lord? Why did He lavish on her such staggering favor? How did she position herself to receive the kind of favor she could scarcely have imagined?

While the Bible never explicitly tells us "why," it does leave us strong clues about how Mary positioned herself to become so "highly favored." And to my eyes, those clues tend to cluster around her faithfulness.

1. She was faithful before she was chosen.

Mary did not become faithful after God chose her as the mother of Jesus. God chose her, in part, because she had already proven herself faithful. Many clues lead us to this conclusion.

First, we know she kept herself sexually pure, for she was a virgin at the time of the angel's visit. Her virginity, in fact, prompted her to ask a very logical question that we'll consider a little later. Second, she calls herself "the Lord's servant,"[4] a role she obviously had taken seriously for some time. Third, she clearly had developed a close relationship with God, for she knew Him by many titles: "the Lord,"[5] "God my Savior,"[6] "the Mighty One,"[7] and "holy."[8] Fourth, she "glorified" God and "rejoiced in" God in a very natural way, characteristic of someone who does such things out of regular habit.[9]

In short, God had been watching this faithful woman for some time. He knew her habits. He knew her spirit. He knew her history. He knew her routines. God knew the pure condition of her heart and that she was faithful to Him *before* He asked her to bear His Son. He knew she would remain faithful to Him *after* He entrusted His Son to her care. Mary's faithfulness powerfully attracted the favorable attention of God.

2. She was faithful after she was chosen.

The angel's shocking appearance and announcement both troubled and frightened Mary, yet nothing that happened that day changed her resolve to remain faithful to God. The angel told her to name her baby "Jesus," and she did so.[10] The law of Moses told her to circumcise her infant on the eighth day; she did so.[11] The law told her how to purify herself and her baby after delivery; she did so.[12] Likewise, God's law instructed her to consecrate her firstborn to the Lord[13] and make some required sacrifices for Him.[14] She did so. Mary trusted in her Lord and believed His words before Gabriel's visit, and she continued to do so afterward.[15]

> MARY SHOWS US THAT FAITH BUILDS MORE FAITH, AND THAT FAITHFULNESS MULTIPLIES FAITHFULNESS.
>
> ♦ ♦ ♦

3. She was faithful in the midst of the unknown.

Mary didn't remain faithful because she understood everything that happened to her. She remained faithful despite her inability to understand.

Have you ever really pondered the angel's answer to her question about how a virgin like her could get pregnant? The angel gives her an answer, but it really doesn't give much of an explanation (other than that a human male would not be involved).

We're dealing in divine mysteries here, and we human beings just don't have the intellectual chops to comprehend the "how." Still, Mary takes the angel at his word (as much of it as she can understand) and replies, *"May it be done to me according to your word."*[16] She doesn't even repeat the angelic "explanation" — she merely replies, "Okay, whatever you say."

Faithful people aren't gullible people nor do they lack all curiosity. While Mary certainly accepted the angel's word even though it still left a lot of things unclear, she apparently had a lifelong habit of turning over in her mind the important issues that she didn't quite understand.

After several shepherds appeared at the birthplace of Jesus to worship the newborn, word of their reports describing singing angels and the birth of the Messiah reached Mary, and the Bible tells us, *"But Mary was treasuring up all these things in her heart and meditating on them."*[17]

Twelve years later, during a family visit to Jerusalem, Mary temporarily lost track of her son and mildly scolded him after she finally located him in the temple. When the young Jesus replied, *"Why were you searching for me? Didn't you know that I had to be in my Father's house?"*[18] The Bible says that neither Mary nor Joseph understood what He meant. But the Scripture then adds, *"His mother kept all these things in her heart."*[19] Even though she was swimming in cosmic waters far too deep for her, she kept on swimming. She remained faithful in the midst of the unknown. And that kind of attitude tends to attract and hold the favorable attention of the Almighty.

4. She was faithful despite the cost.

We've noted before that receiving the favor of God doesn't always mean success in business or trophies in sports or riches in any other life pursuit. It doesn't always mean a large bank account and a swarm of excited admirers. When Mary told the angel, "May it be to me as you have said," she was really saying, "Whatever the cost, I'll be faithful."

There was a cost.

First, what would she tell her fiancé, Joseph? He was no dummy; he clearly had a hard time accepting her explanation that she was pregnant by the Holy Spirit. Matthew's Gospel tells us that Joseph was making plans to quietly end their engagement, when another angelic visit changed his mind.[20]

What would Mary tell her neighbors? Surely the tongues around town started wagging when Mary's stomach began to protrude. As her pregnancy progressed, no doubt Mary had to endure countless looks of disgust and disapproval. Perhaps at times she even blushed, even though she knew the holy truth. For her, the favor of God meant the disfavor of her neighbors.

Did Mary know *"a sword will pierce your own soul"*?[21] Perhaps. We know that when she and her husband went to the temple after the birth of their son, an old man named Simeon prophesied over the child — and not everything he said brought comfort to Mary. Not only did Simeon bless the parents, but he turned to Mary and said specifically to her a veiled reference to the crucifixion some 30-odd years later. So in Mary's case, the favor of God meant a sword thrust into her soul.

Still, Mary remained faithful to her God, all the way to the Cross and to the Resurrection. She stayed faithful to the plan of the gospel, even to the end. She didn't want her Son to die, but even more than that, she wanted what God wanted. She was faithful and highly favored despite the cost.

That didn't mean she was perfect, of course. One infamous time, she and her younger sons and daughters traveled to a house where Jesus had begun to teach, intending to take Him home. Why? According to Mark's Gospel, *"They set out to restrain Him, because they said, 'He is out of His mind.' "*[22]

Perfect? No way. But faithful? No question. Her faithfulness is one big reason why she became so "highly favored" in God's eyes.

Would you, like Mary, choose to remain faithful to God, despite your questions, despite your circumstances, despite the cost? I honestly doubt that many people today would choose to follow Mary's excellent example. In fact, one outspoken woman expressed the modern viewpoint of many when she said, "If I had been the virgin Mary, I would have said 'No.' "[23]

Of course, such a woman would never think of trying to position herself to receive the favor of God. Are you in her insolent camp? Or would you really like to put yourself in the best possible position to receive and enjoy God's favor? If the favor of God is something you desire, then faithfulness ought to occupy a prime spot on your "must have" list.

♦ ♦ ♦ How to Become More Faithful ♦ ♦ ♦

But how can you become more faithful? How can you develop this stellar quality in your own life so that you can increase the likelihood that God will grant you His good favor?

I'd like to suggest five ways to help you become more faithful, and so put yourself in a better position to experience God's wonderful favor. None of them lie beyond your reach, and you can get started on any of them today.

1. See the big picture.

Those who remain faithful to God do so because they see the big picture. They see the end from the beginning. They may not like their current circumstances, but they stick with the Lord because they know that far better things lie ahead.

Such a perspective helps you to take your eyes off the little, annoying things that tend to get you down and, from this perspective, *everything* that's not eternal is "little."

The apostle Paul admitted that he was *"hard pressed on every side,"* *"perplexed,"* *"persecuted,"* *"struck down,"* and even *"always being given over to death,"* and yet he said, *"We do not lose heart."* Why not? Because *"Though outwardly we are wasting away, yet inwardly we are being renewed day by day. For our light and momentary troubles are achieving for us an eternal glory that far outweighs them all."* That's quite a perspective! And how did he manage it? He gave us his secret: *"So we fix our eyes not on what is seen, but on what is unseen. For what is seen is temporary, but what is unseen is eternal."* [24] That's big picture thinking.

We must ask ourselves continually, what is God doing? We must look at the circumstances, as well as what is happening within our own heart. We must gauge various matters, but most of all, we must gauge our faithfulness by the Word of God. Faithfulness to God's Word often quickly appropriates the favor of God.

I believe that one reason why God has so blessed our church is that it has kept the big picture in mind. Our people have been eager to honor the heart of Jesus, which is taking the gospel of Christ to the ends of the earth. God's favor on the church has felt like an irresistible force that opens up closed doors. We can't even keep up with the doors that His favor opens for us.

In the year 2000, I became convinced that something had to expand the borders of our ministry. I believed that we had to build another campus, not to replace the one we had, but to expand the reach of the church. I'd see a bank with many branches in a given geographical area and often wonder, *Why doesn't a church have more than one location in a given area?*

We had noticed that one small region in northwest Arkansas had begun to grow rapidly. After completing a major demographic study and trying to get the heartbeat of what was happening there, we began to build another campus. God's blessing on that work has amazed all of us. What began with 350 of our people, three years later touches over 1,500 people weekly and growing.

2. Remain faithful.

This is such a blessed vision of God. Why? Our church remained faithful to the big picture. God loves to put His favor upon a people committed to take His gospel to the ends of the earth.

We're currently building a 2,400-seat worship center in Pinnacle Hills, and by knocking out two existing walls, we'll end up with 3,800 seats. The completed worship center may become the largest in all of Arkansas. It all began with an impression from the Spirit of God that someone needed to be reached who could not be reached through the ministry of our Springdale campus. It continued to be nurtured by our people, who saw the big picture.

God is accomplishing mighty things by taking a small vision and turning it into a great, strategic ministry. While the Springdale campus will anchor Washington County, the Pinnacle Hills campus will anchor

Benton County. Together, the people in those two locations can do major things for God. All of that is nothing more than the favor of God, poured out due to many expressions of faithfulness informed by the big picture.

Did Mary keep the big picture in mind? She sure did. Her joyful song of praise, recorded in Luke 1:46–55, reveals that she had a kingdom vision. She knew it wasn't about her. She knew it was about God. That's the biggest picture thinking anyone can have.

> GOD TENDS TO PLACE HIS FAVOR ON THOSE WHO TRY TO JOIN WHAT HE'S UP TO.
>
> ◆ ◆ ◆

3. Count your blessings.

Let me ask you: Do you see the big picture? Do you see what God is doing around you? Do you step back to see what the Lord might be doing? Are you faithful to what you see? Faithfulness tends to attract the favor of God. Be faithful to the small things, as well as to the big things. Remember what Jesus said: *"Whoever is faithful in very little is also faithful in much."* [25]

If you want to become more faithful, then remind yourself of the great things God already has done in your life. Dwell on those things. The old hymn is right! When you "count your blessings," you realize how often He's been faithful, and you see how unlikely it would be for Him to stop being faithful. When we ponder how faithful God has been to us, it's a lot easier to remain faithful to Him.

4. Create a family heritage.

Maybe one of those blessings you count is your family heritage. My mother and father raised me to be a godly young man and trained me to get active in a local church. Little did I know, as a boy, that much of my life would be spent in a local church! My mother once told me, "On the Sunday you gave your life to serve God in the ministry, I told Dad, 'We have to give him up.' " So they gave me up. That's the favor of God.

Jeana's mom and dad served in church ministry for many years. In fact, he pastored for about 50 years before he went home to be with the Lord. We should never take our family heritage for granted. Wherever possible, count it as a blessing from God.

Mary did this. She spoke of God's mercy extended to her family members *"from generation to generation,"*[26] and recounted blessings all the way back to her distant ancestors, *"to Abraham and his descendants."*[27] Thinking like that builds personal faithfulness!

Take some time to grab a piece of paper and a pen. Write down every blessing you have ever received, including the blessings you're receiving right now. If you make the effort to do that, you will develop an attitude of gratitude. You will come to recognize blessings you didn't even know you had. It is crucial to take time to thank God for what He's done in us. A grateful heart positions its owner to receive the favor of God.

5. Surround yourself with faithful people of God.

You'll also become more faithful when you stick close to godly men and women who faithfully serve and worship their God. Faithfulness has a way of "rubbing off" on people.

We certainly see this principle at work in the life of Mary. As soon as she heard from Gabriel, she hightailed it to see her cousin, Elizabeth, a godly woman who immediately endorsed Mary's decision to follow God, whatever the cost. Joseph also had to be a great encouragement to her, as were Simeon and an elderly prophetess named Anna.[28] All of these godly people confirmed God's work in Mary's life and helped her to become even more faithful than she had been.

If you want more faith in your life, begin to hang out with people of faith. Begin to learn from the faith of others. You will discover that the favor of God tends to come more frequently when you hang out with the right people — people of great faith. If you want to walk in the land of giants, you need to walk with some giants of faith.

♦♦♦ God Continues to Work in You ♦♦♦

If you want to become more faithful, don't merely look to the past but peer deeply into the present, as well. Don't become the kind of believer who thinks that all of the "good stuff" happened long ago, in the distant past. Train yourself to follow the example of the Psalmist: *"I raise my eyes toward the mountains. Where will my help come from? My help comes from the LORD, the Maker of heaven and earth."*[29]

Realize that God is working on your behalf — right now, at this moment, at this very instant. God is at work in everything that happens to you. God is working on you, even when it feels as though He's far, far away.

Mary had an advantage in this department, of course, since she couldn't help but see God's continued work in her life. As she saw her belly swell and felt the child within move and kick, she remembered that this baby had been placed there by God Almighty. What an encouragement to faithfulness that must have been!

Do not forget that you are a work in progress. The work that God may have begun in you years ago continues today; He really isn't finished with you yet. Be confident that God wants to work in your life. In fact, He *is* working in your life. Every divine favor that you enjoy reveals that God continues to work in your life.

♦♦♦ Be Faithful in the "Little Things" ♦♦♦

Jesus told us, *"Whoever is faithful in very little is also faithful in much, and whoever is unrighteous in very little is also unrighteous in much. So if you have not been faithful with the unrighteous money, who will trust you with what is genuine?"*[30] If you want to grow a big tree of faithfulness, you have to start by planting some little seeds of faithfulness. Do you want to grow in your faithfulness to God? Then start by remaining faithful to the smaller obligations God gives you right now.

I believe one of the reasons God has shown me His favor is that I made some commitments many years ago to remain faithful in some specific ways, both to my wife and to my boys.

Almost 20 years ago I committed to spend every Friday with my wife. I try very hard not to go into the office on Friday, and if I do, I stay only briefly. My goal is to keep from getting tied up at all. I don't break that commitment unless she and I agree that I should. I suspect that God may look on that commitment and say, "Well, Ronnie, you got that one right. Your priorities are where they need to be."

I made a similar commitment to my boys. I didn't want to be one of those absent pastor-fathers who never shows up at a ballgame or some other significant event. One afternoon at a former church, I was going home before I had to return for a deacon's meeting that evening — a meeting that I knew would pack some fireworks. The church had grown explosively, and the power brokers could sense they were losing their control. I knew I was in for a showdown at the OK Corral, so I wanted to get home and see my boys before the bullets started whizzing.

On the ten-minute drive home, it hit me. I will never forget the street I was on and the clear sense that the Lord was speaking to me at the stop sign. At that moment, I made a big-time commitment to the Lord. I said, "Lord, never again will I sacrifice my family on the altar of ministry success." And from that day on, I made sure that I kept that commitment.

Only one time did I miss watching my sons play a ballgame, due to a once-in-a-lifetime ministry opportunity in Washington, DC. Even then, they practically had to pry me loose to get me to go. John Maxwell called to tell me, "Ronnie, it ain't hard. Don't be an idiot. Go!" When I told my boys that they could make the final decision, they said, "Dad, go!"

In a similar vein, Mary spent about 16 years remaining faithful in her commitment to a bunch of "little things" before God entrusted her with the biggest thing of all. The

> MARY NEVER KNEW SHE WAS "IN TRAINING" FOR THE GREATEST ASSIGNMENT OF ANY LIFETIME. LIKEWISE, NEITHER YOU NOR I KNOW WHAT GOD MAY HAVE IN MIND FOR US.
>
> ◆ ◆ ◆

big thing would not have come unless she first had proven her faithfulness in the little things.

Remember this: Mary never knew she was "in training" for the greatest assignment of any lifetime. Likewise, neither you nor I know what God may have in mind for us. But you can be sure He's watching to see how we treat the "little things" He puts in our path!

Those little things may include what you do in your marriage to make it more meaningful. They may involve what you need to do in your job to improve the work climate, or letting someone know that you're grateful for what they do. Giving an unexpected "thank you" to someone who has had a positive impact on your life — perhaps a teacher, or a coach, or a pastor. Maybe only God sees the "little things" you do. Your little acts of obedience go unnoticed by the world.

But you can trust me on this: God's favor tends to run toward those who remain faithful in the little things. So let God's favor run to you today!

♦ ♦ ♦ Bigger Than Giants ♦ ♦ ♦

What's the real connection between faithfulness and receiving God's favor? How are the two connected? The life of Joshua can give us a big clue.

Out of all the guys God could have chosen to lead the nation of Israel into the Promised Land, He chose Joshua. Have you ever wondered why?

For one thing, Joshua had shown his faithfulness. He remained faithful to Moses, as his right-hand man and aide, from the very beginning. He remained faithful when the people grumbled. He remained faithful when ten of his comrades-in-arms made the Israelites quake with fear through their horrific tales of fearsome giants in the land they were supposed to occupy. Sure, Joshua saw the giants, but he remained faithful and saw something bigger and taller and stronger than the giants. He saw God. He walked by faith, and that's why he became an increasingly faithful man. So is it any accident that God showed Him incredible favor? I seriously doubt it.

Would you like to enjoy favor like that? Would you like God's favor to bless the socks off of your life? If so, then I suggest you make a commitment to becoming a faithful man or woman, just as Joshua did.

Things worked out pretty well for him, didn't they?

9 BY KNOWING

Frank Peretti knew something. He just didn't know if anyone else knew. Frank knew that he had a certain facility for writing fiction. He knew that he was a Christian. He knew that Christian fiction was potentially huge in the marketplace.

It was obvious to this admittedly fledgling writer that God wanted him to use his talents to convey truth to a wider world. So Frank wrote. He wrote seemingly as long as it took Noah to build the ark. He wrote between jobs. He wrote at home. He submitted manuscripts, and waited. And waited.

Dozens of publishers turned him down. Then one day, as legend has it, recording artist Amy Grant told a concert audience that they needed to read this great book called This Present Darkness. Pandemonium. Frank's life changed forever. Another book rolled off the presses, then another. Frank Peretti was a certified hit.

It isn't stretching the truth to say that Frank's success paved the way for Christian authors to reach around the globe, with books topping the best-seller lists.

Frank Peretti was faithful to what God wanted him to do, even in the years that were so lean that Frank would disappear if you looked at him sideways. Today, his books are read in airports, board rooms, dens, ballfields . . . everywhere. He knew that he knew.

The story of a man faithful in one thing (perservering in his career), and God enabled something else (a global writing reach) to happen.

♦ ♦ ♦ IF YOU DO X, THEN Y WILL RESULT ♦ ♦ ♦

No one has ever confused me with an astute mathematician. Once I left behind addition, subtraction, multiplication, and division, my level of competency took a quick plunge.

I did learn one principle of mathematics, however, that has served me extremely well in life, including in my study of the Bible. It is called the principle of "If-then." *If* you do X, *then* Y will result.

We see this principle at work all through the Bible. God makes it very clear that *if* His people do A, *then* He will respond with B. Consider 2 Chronicles 7:14, a familiar verse to many: "If *My people who are called by My name humble themselves, pray and seek My face, and turn from their evil ways*, then *I will hear from heaven, forgive their sin, and heal their land*" (emphasis added). When God's people do certain things — in this case, humble themselves, pray, seek His face, and turn from their evil behavior — then God promises to do certain other things — hear their prayers, forgive their sin, and heal their land.

We find the same "if/then" principle in various New Testament passages. In James 4:8, for example, God tells us, *"Draw near to God, and He will draw near to you."* *If* we will draw near to God, *then* God will draw near to us.

The formula is a little more complex when it comes to God's favor, but even here the basic principle holds true. *If* we become the kind of people who increasingly reflect Christ and eagerly do God's will, *then* the Lord is far more likely to visit us with His tremendous good favor.

Now, that's a mathematical formula I can get excited about!

♦ ♦ ♦ TWO FOUNDATION STONES ♦ ♦ ♦

In this final chapter, I want to suggest that receiving the favor of God is built on two crucial foundation stones.

1. The favor of God comes through knowing God.

God created us to be close to Him, to enjoy a deep and rich and loving relationship with Him. In that regard, the Lord of the universe asks us an intriguing question in Jeremiah 30:21: *"For who would otherwise risk his life to approach Me? This is the LORD's declaration."*

I've been thinking a lot lately about God's question. Who *will* devote himself to be close to the Lord? Will I? Will you?

It's not an idle question, for the Scriptures suggest that God is most likely to bestow His blessing on those who, more than anything else, want to know *Him*. God loves to send His best favor on those who want *God* more than they want any of His blessings.

Herein lies one of the great problems for many contemporary followers of Christ. Many of us busily seek the hands of God — what He can do for us — rather than seek the face of God, for who He is. *"He revealed His ways to Moses,"* says Psalm 103:7, *"His deeds to the people of Israel."* While Moses knew the ways of God — that is, His habits, His heart, His face — the people of Israel settled merely for His deeds, His acts, His hands. With Moses, God would speak "face to face," as with a friend; but the Israelites constantly sought what God could do for them, and many times, even the latest and greatest miracle was not enough to satisfy them.

Psalm 103:7 reminds us that it is far more important to understand God's ways than it is to know God's acts. His hands are wonderful, but His face is infinitely better.

So what does it mean to know God? What does it mean to enjoy personal intimacy with the Lord of glory? All the great people of the Scripture knew God in an intimate way. Whether you think of Abel, Noah, Abraham, Joseph, Moses, Joshua, Caleb, Ruth, Deborah, David, Jonathan, and Esther in the Old Testament, or John, Peter, Mary, Martha, Paul, Priscilla, and Aquila in the New Testament, you bring to mind men and women who knew and loved God for who He is, not merely for what He could do for them. Church history since Bible times confirms how God's favor consistently comes in power on certain men and women, on faithful believers such as Augustine and Martin Luther and Fanny Crosby and Catherine Marshall.

But why did it come? Why did the favor of God settle on the lives of these people?

They all knew and loved God!

I want to know God like they did. I want to walk along intimate pathways with Him, to get to know His heart, to see His face. That's why I feel so strongly about rising early in the morning, as often as possible, to start my day with God. I simply *must* get to know Him.

I have walked with the Lord long enough to understand that His favor most often comes through knowing Him. By spending time with Him I do not merely seek His favor (although that is an excellent route to it), because I recognize that the privilege of knowing Him intimately is itself the greatest favor of all.

So how does one come to know God? Let me suggest a few things that I have seen through the years as a Christian and as a Christian leader that determine whether a person takes steps to get to know God better.

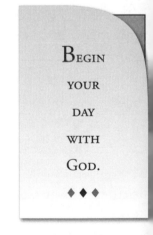

Begin
your
day
with
God.
♦ ♦ ♦

- *Put Christ first every day.* Begin your day with God. Put Him first, not only in your family life, but also in your business and in your career. Of course, it's pretty hard to place Him first if He's never come into your life! So if you have never received Christ, open your heart right now and let Jesus come in. That decision should begin a habit of daily placing Christ first in your life. God's favor tends to fall mightily on those who every day place Christ first in their life.

- *Place the Word of God in yourself every day.* It is imperative that every Christian read the Bible, study the Bible, meditate on the Bible, and learn what the Bible says. This is God's roadmap for a successful life. A new translation of the Scriptures, the Holman Christian Standard Bible, came out recently. Outstanding evangelical scholars from across the world spent years of meticulous study to produce this outstanding Bible version. In the year 2005, we distributed thousands of copies to people in our church. More than 4,000 of them took the challenge to read the Bible through in one year, using a reading plan crafted for our fellowship. We have seen changed lives as a result. Place the Word of God in yourself daily! You position yourself to receive the favor of God when you place the Word of God in your heart every day.

- *Fellowship every week with a Bible-teaching, ministry-driven, evangelistic local church.* It is very difficult to know God in an intimate way without fellowshiping with other believers on a weekly basis, for the purpose of studying God's Word in worship, winning people to Jesus Christ, and ministering to those in the community and across the world. After the 2005 tsunami disaster, we saw churches across America mobilize and provide humanitarian and spiritual aid to victims of the tragedy. God's favor tends to rest on those who fellowship each week with a Bible-teaching, evangelistic, ministry-driven local church.

- *Serve God every month by doing some specific ministry.* God has gifted you to do something for Him. He has equipped you in a tangible way to serve Him. Discover your giftedness, then share it with a fellowship of local believers, and then join in partnership with them, at least once every month. The favor of God tends to greatly bless those who serve Him regularly through some specific ministry.

- *Do your part to help fulfill the Great Commission.* Christians today need to see the big picture and get beyond themselves. One way to do this is to engage with those who do not yet have a relationship with Christ. Also, if we want to develop a Christian world view, we need to expose ourselves to people worldwide and learn how to minister to them. Consider going on a short-term mission trip once every five years. Allow God to use your life to minister to people across the world, especially to those who do not yet know Christ. I have learned through the years that God's favor tends to run to those who engage in fulfilling the Great Commission.

2. The favor of God comes through knowing His will and doing it.

All great men and women of faith have a passion to discover God's will and do it. They show us that the favor of God tends to fall most often, most powerfully, and most delightfully upon men and women who know the Lord intimately and who yearn to know His will and then do it. It is not enough simply to know what God wants us to do; we must also do it, through the power of God's Spirit.

Many people through the years have asked me, "But how do I know God's will?" Along the way I have observed that three things occur in my life when I sense that God is leading me to do something.

First, there is *initiation*. God initiates what He wants us to do. He begins the process, not you or I. Remember, it's not about me promoting me, it's about me following God. So I look around to see what God seems to be doing. When I sense that God may be initiating this or that circumstance, my challenge is not only to understand what He may be doing, but to remain willing to conform my life to His activity.

Second, I have to learn to recognize God's *timing*. God has a strong commitment to a divine timetable. He does things at just the right moment.[1] God is never too early, nor is He ever late. He is always right on time.

When I see what God is doing and sense that He wants me to join Him in it, I have to ask myself, *Is this the right time? Is this God's timing for me to do this?* It doesn't matter whether the thing involves ministry or day-to-day life, the question remains the same. We need to learn to do the right thing at the right time — God's time.

Third, I must be *willing*. Jesus made a very interesting comment in the fifth chapter of John's Gospel. He said He reveals His will to *those willing to do it.* He opens up His heart and His mind to those who show an eager willingness to do whatever He asks them to do. So if you want to know God's will, you must join the "Just Say Yes Club" to God.

All of history's great men and women of faith, whether in the Old Testament or the New Testament or in church history or today built their lives on these two foundation stones. They got to know God intimately, and then they willingly abandoned their own plans and desires in order to do God's will, whatever it might be. They also had something else in common: they all experienced God's favor in abundance.

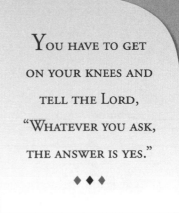

YOU HAVE TO GET ON YOUR KNEES AND TELL THE LORD, "WHATEVER YOU ASK, THE ANSWER IS YES."

♦ ♦ ♦

Would you like to experience the same kind of favor? You can put yourself in a great position to do just that — if you follow the same path they did. Just say yes to God! Favor tends to come in abundance to those who learn to say yes to God.

♦ ♦ ♦ MOSES LEARNS ABOUT FAVOR ♦ ♦ ♦

No discussion about the favor of God would be complete without considering Moses. Without question, Moses enjoyed the enormous favor of God. In fact, from the very beginning of his remarkable life, God gave Moses tremendous, powerful, divine favor.

I think it might help to do a quick "walk through" of Moses' life, to learn some important lessons about the favor of God. I'd like to highlight eight of these lessons that I consider especially meaningful to our own lives.

1. God's favor protects.

Moses' mother, fearing for his young life, placed her infant son inside a reed basket and floated him down the Nile River. Before long, a young Egyptian woman noticed the odd basket, opened it, and took Moses out of the water. So God moved to protect Moses' life in a very unusual (but effective) way. Even more unusual, the man who ordered that all Hebrew baby boys be slaughtered, provided the very household where Moses grew up!

Why did this happen? Mark it up to the favor of God. God showed Moses His favor by protecting him from the king's deadly edict. Why did Moses escape death when so many other cute Hebrew infants did not? For no other reason than that he enjoyed the favor of God.

When you have the favor of God, you have God's protection, as we already saw from Psalm 5:12: *"For You, LORD, bless the righteous one; You surround him with your favor like a shield."* God's favor is like a shield surrounding you.

Jeana and I have seen this through the years. We have seen God protect Jeana through the diagnosis of cancer. We have seen God protect me from unfair and untrue accusations. We have seen God protect our children while children all around us fell into great hardship and tragedy. We have seen God protect our church in adverse times when we penetrated the decaying culture around us. God's favor protects.

2. God's favor prepares.

Moses grew up in the house of Pharaoh, the most powerful man in Egypt. In that house, he learned about the fine points of Egyptian culture and how to conduct himself appropriately. During that time, Moses apparently did not know he was an Israelite. But as he submitted to those in authority over him, God used the house of Pharaoh to prepare him for great future leadership.

When Moses made a huge mistake one day, he had to flee for his life into the desert, where he remained for the next 40 years. It became his extended classroom.

Moses' life is all about preparation. He spent 40 years preparing in the house of Pharaoh, and then he spent another 40 years in the desert of Midian. Before God ever did anything with him publicly, Moses spent two-thirds of his life in preparation for the final, dramatic moment of leadership. It's much like that still today.

I will never forget my young friend Brad Jurkovich, who felt torn about whether to pursue his Masters of Divinity degree. He called to ask my opinion as his pastor, and I strongly encouraged him to enroll at seminary to prepare him for pastoring a church. I also suggested that he sit down with the president of the seminary, a godly man named Dr. Paige Patterson. Brad took my advice and promptly made an appointment to see Dr. Patterson, who spoke with him about the value of preparation. During part of the conversation, Dr. Patterson reached back, gave Brad a small pail full of sand, and told him to carry it around for the next several days as he prayed about what God wanted him to do. Every time Brad looked at it, he was to ask himself, "Am I better than Moses? Why should I not prepare? Moses prepared in the sandy desert for 40 years."

In the end, Brad did go after his master's degree. (After that, who wouldn't?) And today he is in the final stages of working on his Doctor of Ministry degree.

Do you want to enjoy God's favor? Then don't skimp on the preparation!

3. God's favor involves process.

Years ago I came across a powerful statement: "Process always precedes the product." If we want a different product, then we need to stick with the necessary process.

Receiving the favor of God involves a process. So many of us want the *product* of God's favor without going through the *process* to receive it. The great news is that you can grow in the favor of God. You can mature in the favor of God. As you follow God, the process increasingly prepares you to receive greater measures of God's favor.

God took Moses through a lengthy process, from protecting him as a baby, to raising him in the household of Pharaoh, and eventually to placing him in the desert for 40 years — all to prepare him for one shining moment of historic leadership. Even when God called Moses back to Egypt, the process continued. Moses clearly did not want to accept the position to which God had called him. He made every excuse he could think of to explain why he could not be the best man for the job. His calling involved a process, as did his submission to that calling.

One day a few years ago, a young, successful, sharp, and good-looking guy named John David Lindsey walked into my office. I may have met John David somewhere along the way, but if I had, I didn't remember it. He told me that he had been away from God, but he wanted to come back. John David was not a member of our fellowship, but he had started to attend after he began dating a lady from our church. He was 30-something, never married, prosperous, and from a family that had done well. He told me that he had been coming to hear God's Word — and then he quoted much of what I had said in the previous few weeks.

In time, John David married his lovely wife, Amy. God has blessed them in many ways. John David took over a successful real estate company and turned it into the number one company in all of Arkansas. Even as a young man, he was on his way to incredible blessing. He has since become a good friend, and I have noticed that as he cleaned up his life through the power of God's Holy Spirit and committed himself to God's work, the Lord has showered him with His favor. Today, John David has the potential to become a major difference maker in the realm of business throughout the state of Arkansas. Why is this?

> NEVER FORGET IT: GOD'S FAVOR TYPICALLY INVOLVES A PROCESS — A PROCESS OF BECOMING MORE LIKE CHRIST.
>
> ◆ ◆ ◆

John David went through a process in which God got him where He wanted him. Now it's a process of keeping him where God wants him. He went through a process of learning what it means to be truly successful in business. He went through a process of learning what it means to become all that God wants him to become. John David is like all of us. He has a long way to go. But when he calls me, he always says, "Keep the dream alive." John David is able to dream big because he has learned more about process than ever before. I have learned something through the years: God's favor always follows healthy process. When someone processes his or her life, tries to get it right, makes it right, and carries out steps to ensure that it stays right, God tends to lavish His favor upon that person.

When I think of John David Lindsey, I think of Psalm 90:17: *"Let the favor of the Lord our God be on us; establish for us the work of our hands — establish the work of our hands."* This young man has the favor of the Lord upon him, and every day God is establishing the work of his hands.

Do you want God's favor? Then expect to go through a process. Not one of us can escape going through that process.

4. God's favor promotes.

When God's time came to promote Moses, Moses didn't want the job. He certainly didn't go to "GreatJobs.com" and see that the Lord needed someone to free the people of Israel from the tyranny of the Egyptians! In fact, Moses did everything he could to escape what God wanted him to do — until finally he understood that God had been setting him up for this very thing all of his life.

We must never forget that *God* laid on Moses the mantle of leadership. He didn't receive it from a committee of men or women, nor from the leaders of Israel, nor from his friends and associates, nor from his family. God laid the mantle of leadership upon Moses. God took this man, weak in so many ways, and made him strong enough to stand in the very presence of Pharaoh and declare the Word of the Lord. You know that famous word: *"Let my people go!"* [2]

Even though Moses felt very reluctant to pick up the leadership mantle, he finally did it because he knew that's what God wanted. His face-to-face encounter with God on the mountain made it impossible for him to walk away.

Have you had such an encounter? Are you coming to know God, face-to-face? If so, don't feel surprised when God's favor promotes you to something unexpected. It's happened before!

5. God's favor has a plan.

When the favor of God comes upon your life, you begin to live life by a different plan. You don't arrive at that plan by hammering it out on a retreat, nor do you devise it as you drive down the road. God himself reveals that plan to you — maybe at a retreat, maybe while you drive down the road, but *He* initiates it, not you or I.

I suspect that Moses would have felt very content to stay the rest of his life in the desert; he'd already made it his home for 40 years. But from the day he said "yes" to God, he began to understand the big picture. He began to see, not the obstacles or the inadequacies or weaknesses of his personality, but the big picture, namely, that God wanted him to return to his birthplace and there declare to Pharaoh, "Let my people go." He knew that God's plan called for freeing the Israelites from the bondage of the Egyptians. He also knew that God's perfect plan called for him to lead more than two million Israelites out of Egypt and into the Promised Land.

> GOD HAS A BIG PLAN FOR YOUR LIFE AND ONLY HE KNOWS HOW THAT PLAN WILL UNFOLD.
>
> ◆ ◆ ◆

Try your best to begin to see the big picture. The big picture is God's picture about you, not your picture about yourself. But you will begin to see God's plan a lot better when you begin to see the big picture.

Let me ask: What is God's plan for you? What parts of that plan has He already shown you by His favor? If you want to get in line for God's favor, you need to get aligned with His plan.

6. God's favor leads to proclamation.

As soon as Moses knew what God wanted him to do, he proclaimed it unashamedly to his people. He did not show hesitancy nor feel embarrassed about what God wanted him to do. Just as Noah proclaimed that a flood was coming to a people who never understand the concept of rain, so Moses announced to Pharaoh, "Let my people go." This took enormous courage. It took God-sized faith to proclaim that the time had come to leave Egypt and follow God into the Promised Land, where milk and honey flowed like swift-running rivers.

Are you ashamed of what God is doing in your life? Or do you love to proclaim it whenever you get the chance? Those who proclaim what the favor of God already has accomplished in their lives tend to see even more of that favor.

7. God's favor brings power.

Moses saw the mighty power of God. He did not lead Israel in his own power, nor did the strength of his arm perform any of the great acts that rocked the Israelites. Moses saw the power of God and experienced the miracles of God. Through God's power, the plagues of God fell upon the Egyptians. Through the power of God, the Israelites followed a pillar of cloud by day and a pillar of fire by night. God used His power to bring lifestyle change not only to Moses, but to the lives of countless thousands of Israelites.

Moses saw the power of God in all kinds of circumstances. When the Israelites looked hopelessly trapped between the Red Sea on one side and an attacking Egyptian army on the other, God made a highway through the sea for two million Hebrews to cross to safety. When Korah and his clan stood up to oppose Moses, God demonstrated His power by causing the earth to open up beneath Korah's feet, sending him alive into the depths of the earth. Moses saw miracle after miracle.

When you receive God's favor, you also will see God's power in staggering ways. Do you need that power in your life? Do you need to be released from some terrible bondage? Then position yourself to receive the favor of God. Favor is power. Ask for it. Wait for it. And then stand back and enjoy the show.

8. God's favor has a personal aspect.

Beyond all doubt, Moses enjoyed the favor of God — and because he received it, so did the people around him. The whole Hebrew nation got blessed because of the favor shown to Moses. That means the favor of God carries great responsibility.

Do you remember when Moses grew so angry with his people that, contrary to what God had instructed, he struck a rock with his staff rather than speaking to it? His sin cost him greatly. Because of it, God would not allow Moses to cross into the Promised Land with the nation.

But Moses recovered from his disappointment. He came back from his failure. He dealt with it. He lived with it. Still, the merciful God of heaven showed Moses His favor. Before Moses died, God sent him to the top of a mountain to peer into the land of promise.[3] Why? God's favor. When Moses died, God buried him.[4] The Lord gave him a special grave site known only to heaven. That is favor above favor. But even that was not the end! The New Testament tells us that God finally did bring Moses into the Promised Land, at an invitation-only meeting with Elijah the prophet and Jesus the Savior of the world.[5] Favor upon favor upon favor. God gave him all of this, even though he messed up (and did so publicly).

> I WONDER WHAT WE'D SEE IF GOD TOOK US UP ON A MOUNTAIN TO SHOW US THE FAVOR THAT WE MISS BY OUR OWN DISOBEDIENCE?
>
> ◆ ◆ ◆

I wonder what we'd see if God took *us* up on a mountain to show us the favor that we miss by our own disobedience? It would astound us and break our hearts to know how much of God's favor we are missing. Yet, grace covers it all. God still promises us an unbelievable life, not only here, but in eternity.

All because of the favor of God!

Moses knew how to ask for God's favor, even in dark times. When he came down from the mountain to give his people the law of God, he found them running amok — getting drunk, accosting each other, committing vile sexual acts, and worst of all, worshiping a deaf and mute idol. God threatened to put an end to all of them. But then Moses, the man who knew and loved God's favor, petitioned his Lord for that favor. The Bible says simply, *"But Moses sought the favor of the LORD his God."* [6]

Moses knew and loved God's favor, and the more of that favor he had, the more of it he wanted. At one point he reminded the Lord, *"Look, You have told me, 'Lead this people. . . . You said, 'I know you by name and you have also found favor in My sight.' "*And then he added a request: *"Now if I have indeed found favor in Your sight, please teach me Your ways and I will know You and find favor in Your sight."*[7]

Teach me Your ways. . . .

Let me know You. . . .

Let me continue to find favor with You. . . .

More than anything, Moses wanted to know God. He wanted to know God's ways. And because he had experienced some of God's favor, he asked for even more.

What about you?

Have you messed up? Have you blown it? Do you think you're not worthy of God's favor upon you? Listen, we have all blown it. It does not matter what sin you may have committed or how you have disappointed your family or how you have neglected God. Today is a new day. This moment is a new moment. God's favor has a personal aspect. Once we deal with our mistakes, personal dynamics beyond belief kick in. They may show themselves through blessings, through provision, through protection, or in any number of other ways. But rest assured that you are not outside of God's grace and God's favor. Just as He gave Moses the privilege of looking into the Promised Land, so He gives you the privilege of coming to know Christ intimately. That is your Promised Land. That is where you discover real, awesome, even breathtaking favor.

♦ ♦ ♦ THE FAVOR OF GOD AND YOU ♦ ♦ ♦

Have you ever seen God protect you? Do you realize that every day of your life, He protects you from terrible things you never even see? God protects those who know and love Him. Sometimes, He even protects you from yourself. I know that I can be my biggest enemy!

God's favor is protecting you right now. Even if you're lying in a hospital bed, God is protecting you. Even if you're walking through financial loss or bankruptcy, God is protecting you. Even if you have lost your job, God is protecting you. Each time you see God protecting you, that is His favor. Jude 1 reminds you that you are kept in Jesus Christ. The Lord guards you and protects you in all matters of life. God's protection comes for one reason alone: God's favor. Thank God today for His favor of protection.

Have you ever sensed God preparing you for something? Our God does a great job at preparing us. He prepares us for future success. He prepares us through adversity. Our God is always preparing us for something.

Your Lord uses all the events of your life to prepare you for the ultimate event: that awesome time when you meet Him face to face. The faith He creates in you now will be the faith that gets you through on the day you die. I will never forget what my professor, Dr. Oscar Thompson, said years ago in a class on evangelism. "Dying grace," he said, "comes only to a dying man. You don't need dying grace until you die."

Everything that God does in you and for you and around you gets you ready for that ultimate challenge of death. But until then, He is preparing you for something great in this life. Be comforted today, for God's favor is preparing you.

Have you ever sensed that God wanted to mature you in some area? I believe we have all felt that, even though sometimes we ignore it. God's favor has a way of constantly moving you toward the likeness of Jesus Christ. He is like a sculptor who looks at a piece of stone and chips away everything that does not look like the finished piece he has in mind. God is chipping off the areas of your life that do not look like Christ. It is God's favor that makes us more like Christ.

Has something really great ever happened to you that you had nothing to do with? Could it be that God is promoting you? Could it be that God has decided to get the forces of heaven behind you? Can you imagine the God of heaven deciding to support your cause? When He does, not one opponent can stand in your way. Nothing can keep you down. His favor has a way of promoting you. You can go further with God's favor than you could ever go just on your own ability or contacts. God has a way of lifting up those with a humble heart.

Have you ever been able to see the big picture of what's going on in your life? That big picture comes because of the favor of God. Several times I've reminded you that God has a plan for your life. It's a great plan designed to mold you into the likeness of Christ. That plan will have ups and downs, mountains and valleys, victories and setbacks. It's all God's plan. The greatest way to enjoy God's favor is to cooperate with His plan for your life. Learn what He is trying to do with you, through you, and around you, then adapt your behavior to what you sense God is doing with your life. Finding a true direction for life is a result of God's favor in your life.

Have you ever had the courage to declare what you know God wants you to do, even when it doesn't make sense? That kind of courage comes by the favor of God. Never feel ashamed to declare what the Lord is doing in you. If He's the one doing it, it's not pride or ego to declare it. Rather, it's a testimony about God and the great things He's doing. People need to know that our God is alive and active and involved in your life. When they sense that God is vitally involved in your life, they will want to know more about what they sense in you. When you have boldness that seems to come out of nowhere or courage that surprises you, remember this: it's all God's favor. Shout it from the mountaintops. It's the favor of God!

Have you ever seen God move in your life in a powerful way, perhaps even with a miracle or two? That's not only possible, it's probable with the favor of God. I believe with all my heart that God wants to do so many things around us and through us, if we would just surrender to Him, place ourselves in the right spot, seek Him and receive His favor. Then we will see God do amazing things. The God of Abraham, the God of Moses, the God of Elijah, the God of John, the God of Paul is alive. He is the same God yesterday, today, and forever. And He loves to shower His people with powerful expressions of His favor. Can you imagine having the steady, loving gaze of God on your life? Let His gaze fix upon you.

Have you ever sensed that you're special, that something's unique about you? That is favor. God is mightily involved in your life, through all of your failures, disappointments, and even in your discouragement. God is involved. He wants to lift you up, reignite you, and get you back on a route that destines you for greatness. The only way you can ever be put back together, however, is through the favor of God. Forgiveness is favor. A second chance is favor. Starting over is favor. Make your decision today and say, "I choose the favor of God."

My friend, this is not simply the favor of man; this is the favor of God — and how He wants to shower it upon your life. Your job is to position yourself for it, even as Moses did.

♦ ♦ ♦ Spell It F-A-V-O-R ♦ ♦ ♦

Let me give you something to remember. It is simple, but potent.

F — Favor. God loves to smile upon His obedient children.

A — Always. The favor of God affirms His touch on our life.

V — Verifies. Nothing shows our connection to God more than His favor.

O —Our. Favor has a deeply personal aspect.

R — Relationship. God waits to enjoy a heart-to-heart connection with you on a daily basis, so that He can change you into something great.

So get the message of the acrostic. **Favor Always Verifies Our Rela**tionship to God. Our families need to see it. Our work associates need to see it. Our friends need to see it. Our neighbors need to see it. Our culture needs to see it. The world needs to see the favor of God upon His children. Why? Because His favor always verifies our relationship to God. It truly shows that my life is not about me, but about something far greater than me. It's about God.

I suffered through a lot of hot, humid southwest Texas days during my teenage years. On those days I used to wonder, *Where am I going? What will I do?* All I knew is that God was doing something new in me. I recognized that I had begun a great adventure.

But I had no idea how great it would be.

As I look back over my life, I believe the following three words capture the essence of what has happened to me: *Favored by God.*

Please don't misunderstand. I'm not talking about favor that I earned or deserved. I'm talking about God's gracious favor, bestowed on me out of His heart of love. Just as God has chosen to demonstrate His favor in my life, in my family, and in my career, He wants to do the same thing for you. But you must first position yourself well to receive His favor. You must choose to live in such a way that God will take great pleasure in setting His loving gaze upon you.

To some degree, God's favor is *always* on those who know Christ. But something powerful happens when He sets His gaze upon you to show you His special favor. It's like a basketball player who's "in the zone," and everything he shoots drops through the net. It's like a quarterback who completes every pass he throws. It's like a business person who turns everything he or she touches into gold. It's like a mom who raises nothing but presidents and supreme court justices.

But I'm talking here about something far greater than a game, or a business, or even our kids. I'm talking about the favor of God. I challenge you: Do not settle for mediocrity! Do not settle for silence when God wants to give you peace. Do not settle for indifference when God wants to give you joy. Do not settle for so little when God wants to give you so much!

For the next month, I want to challenge you to end every day with a prayer for the favor of God. At the close of this book, you will see a list of my top 10 Bible verses on the favor of God. As you pray every day for the favor of God on your life, interweave some of these great promises concerning His favor.

His favor is waiting for you.

For the next month, I want to challenge you to begin every day:

> Lord, I seek You and want to know You. I cannot go anywhere and enjoy ultimate success without the favor of God. I ask you today for the favor of God to fall upon me and my family. I ask for the favor of God upon all my relationships. I ask for the favor of God upon my career. Please set your loving gaze upon me, and get all the forces of heaven behind me because of Your mercy and grace. Help me to get myself into position to receive the awesome favor of God. May your favor be a testimony of my relationship to you. In Jesus' name, Amen.

Pray for the favor of God every day. And when you do, things will never be the same.

Join me in this marvelous adventure that God has in store for both of us — an adventure powered by His amazing favor.

What words can be said to bring closure to such a life-changing subject? I think one of my heroes has a word for us, a word for me. He was one of the greatest leaders of all time. Out of all ways he could have closed his book, he closed it this way. In the same manner, I close my book with this humble, but fervent, passionate request for you and for me:

Remember me, my God, with favor (Neh. 13:31).

Favorite Verses on the Favor of God

Then the king responded to the man of God, "Please plead for the favor of the LORD your God and pray for me so that my hand may be restored to me." So the man of God pleaded for the favor of the LORD, and the king's hand was restored to him and became as it had been at first (1 Kings 13:6).

When he was in distress, he sought the favor of the LORD his God and earnestly humbled himself before the God of his ancestors (2 Chron. 33:12).

I also arranged for the donation of wood at the appointed times and for the firstfruits. Remember me, my God, with favor (Neh. 13:31).

God is not partial to princes and does not favor the rich over the poor, for they are all the work of His hands (Job 34:19).

But as for me, LORD, my prayer to You is for a time of favor. In Your abundant, faithful love, God, answer me with Your sure salvation (Ps. 69:13).

Restore us, LORD God of Hosts; look [on us] with favor, and we will be saved (Ps. 80:19).

Let the favor of the Lord our God be on us; establish for us the work of our hands — establish the work of our hands! (Ps. 90:17).

Then you will find favor and high regard in the sight of God and man (Prov. 3:4).

Therefore, our God, hear the prayer and the petitions of Your servant. Show Your favor to Your desolate sanctuary for the Lord's sake (Dan. 9:17).

And now ask for God's favor. Will He be gracious to us? [Since] this has come from your hands, will He show any of you favor?" asks the LORD of Hosts (Mal. 1:9).

ENDNOTES

Chapter 1
1. Genesis 4:3–5; NIV.
2. 1 John 3:12.
3. Matthew 23:35; Hebrews 11:4.
4. Genesis 6:8.
5. Genesis 6:9.
6. Luke 1:25.
7. Luke 2:52.
8. Psalm 84:11.
9. Psalm 90:17.
10. Genesis 39:21.
11. Psalm 5:12.
12. Exodus 32:7–14; 33:12–23.
13. Ezra 7:27–28.
14. 1 Samuel 16:1–13.
15. Acts 7:46.
16. 2 Samuel 7:8–16.
17. 2 Samuel 12:7-12.
18. 2 Samuel 12:16–17.
19. 2 Samuel 12:22.
20. 2 Samuel 12:20.
21. 1 Samuel 13:14; Acts 13:22; NIV.
22. 2 Corinthians 1:10–12; NIV, emphasis added.

Chapter 2
1. Daniel 4:35
2. Revelation 4:8
3. Isaiah 22:22; Revelation 3:7
4. Galatians 4:4–5
5. 2 Samuel 7:3
6. 1 Kings 8:18–19
7. 2 Samuel 7:18, 19, 22, 28, 29
8. Isaiah 14:27
9. Psalm 33:10–11
10. Colossians 2:19
11. Daniel 9:13; NIV
12. Daniel 9:17

Chapter 3
1. Romans 11:25; NIV
2. 1 Corinthians 15:51–52
3. Ephesians 3:4–6
4. Colossians 1:27
5. Ephesians 5:32
6. Matthew 19:30
7. John 21:20–22
8. Isaiah 55:9
9. Psalm 97:2
10. Deuteronomy 29:29
11. 2 Kings 4:27
12. Psalm 10:1
13. Job 13:24
14. 1 Chronicles 11:19
15. Acts 15:26; Romans 16:4; Philippians 2:30
16. 1 Corinthians 2:9
17. Ruth 2:10; NIV
18. Hebrews 10:36
19. James 1:4

Chapter 4
1. Matthew 7:7
2. Genesis 32:24-30; Hosea 12:4
3. Jeremiah 26:19
4. Daniel 9:17
5. Nehemiah 5:19
6. Nehemiah 13:31
7. 2 Kings 13:4
8. 2 Chronicles 33:12–13
9. 2 Chronicles 33:9
10. Genesis 39:2
11. Genesis 39:5
12. Genesis 39:21
13. Genesis 41:1
14. James 4:14
15. Jude 14–15
16. Hebrews11:5
17. Genesis 5:22, 24
18. Deuteronomy 33:13–16
19. Genesis 50:25; Exodus 13:19; Joshua 24:32

Chapter 5
1. James 1:17; NIV
2. Matthew 5:45

3. Acts 14:17; NIV
4. Haggai 2:8
5. Lamentations 3:31–33
6. James 1:17
7. 2 Corinthians 9:11; NIV
8. 1 Timothy 6:6–8
9. 1 Corinthians 14:33
10. Nehemiah 1:11; NIV
11. Nehemiah 5:19; 13:31
12. Matthew 19:26

Chapter 7
1. Luke 2:52
2. 1 Samuel 2:26
3. Jeremiah 15:1
4. Exodus 33:11
5. 1 Samuel 1:27–28
6. 1 Samuel 2:18
7. 1 Samuel 2:21
8. 1 Samuel 2:35
9. 1 Samuel 3:2–18
10. John 14:23
11. 1 Samuel 2:26
12. 2 Peter 3:18
13. Matthew 15:19
14. Isaiah 57:15
15. 1 Corinthians 3:18–21
16. James 4:10
17. 1 Peter 5:6
18. Luke 10:38–42
19. Romans 14:23
20. Matthew 28:19–20, emphasis added
21. 2 Corinthians 12:9
22. 2 Corinthians 12:9
23. Jeremiah 29:13
24. Matthew 5:6
25. Psalm 42:1
26. Psalm 5:3; 55:17; 59;16; 88:13
27. Mark 1:35; Luke 5:16
28. John 4:34
29. John 5:30
30. Ephesians 5:25–32

Chapter 8
1. Luke 1:28; NIV
2. Luke 1:30; NIV

3. Luke 1:43
4. Luke 1:38; NIV
5. Luke 1:38, 46
6. Luke 1:47
7. Luke 1:49
8. Luke 1:49
9. Luke 1:46–47
10. Luke 1:31; 2:21
11. Luke 2:21
12. Luke 2:22
13. Luke 2:23
14. Luke 2:24
15. Luke 1:38, 45
16. Luke 1:38
17. Luke 2:19
18. Luke 2:49
19. Luke 2:51
20. Matthew 1:18–25
21. Luke 2:35
22. Mark 3:21
23. Stevie Smith in *The Portable Curmudgeon Redux*, Jon Winokur, editor (New York: Dutton, 1992), p. 312.
24. 2 Corinthians 4:8–16; NIV
25. Luke 16:10
26. Luke 1:50
27. Luke 1: 55
28. Luke 2:36
29. Psalm 121:1–2
30. Luke 16:10–11

Chapter 9
1. See Galatians 4:4; Romans 5:6; Revelation 6:11
2. Exodus 5:1; 7:16; 8:1; 8:20; 9:1; 9:13
3. Deuteronomy 34:1–4
4. Deuteronomy 34:6
5. Matthew 17:1–8
6. Exodus 32:11; NIV
7. Exodus 33:12–13

MORE RESOURCES FROM
DR. RONNIE W. FLOYD

Sermon series:

- Finding the Favor of God
- DNA of the New Testament Church
- Family Life Illustrated

Available on CD/Cassette/VHS/DVD
& transcripts at
www.invitationtolife.org

Other Books by Dr. Floyd
The Gay Agenda
Life on Fire
How to Pray
Family Life Illustrated (set of 6)

TELEVISION • RADIO • INTERNET
Program: *Invitation to Life with Dr. Ronnie Floyd*

TELEVISION
Sundays (7:30 a.m. CST)
WGN Superstation
Wednesdays (8:00 p.m. CST)
Church Channel
Thursdays (9:00 p.m. CST)
Daystar Christian
Television Network

RADIO
Monday – Friday (12:30 p.m. CST)
Calvary Satellite Network
Locate a station at www.csnradio.com

INTERNET
Sundays: (9:15 a.m. CST)
Live webcast on www.fbcs.net

For more information on all resources: www.invitationtolife.org
For information about Dr. Floyd's church:
www.fbcs.net   www.churchph.com
or call (479) 751-4523 and ask for Invitation to Life

Also by Dr. Floyd . . .

FAMILY LIFE
ILLUSTRATED SERIES

Easy-to-study series packed with practical information for keeping your marriage, family, and children balanced.

5 x 7 casebound • 96 pages each
$8.99 ($12.99 CAN)

Men: 0-89221-584-4
Women: 0-89221-583-6
Marriage: 0-89221-585-2
Teens: 0-89221-586-0
Finances: 0-89221-587-9
Parents: 0-89221-588-7
Study Guide: 0-89221-599-2

Available at Christian bookstores nationwide